STANDING FIRM

RECLAIMING CHRISTIAN FAITH
IN TIMES OF CONTROVERSY

PARKER T. WILLIAMSON

PLC Publications

©1996 PLC Publications

PLC Publications
PO Box 2210
136 Tremont Park Drive
Lenoir NC 28645

Unless otherwise noted, Scripture taken from the New King James Version Copyright ©1979, 1980, 1982, Thomas Nelson Inc., Publishers. Used by permission. All rights reserved.

Excerpts from *A New Eusebius* used by permission of SPCK Publishers.

Cover design by E.B. Wall & Associates

ISBN 0-9652602-0-8
Library of Congress Catalogue Number 96-68692

First printing June 1996
Second Printing September 1996

PRINTED IN THE UNITED STATES OF AMERICA

FOR MY PARENTS
RENÉ AND VIRGINIA WILLIAMSON

CONTENTS

PREFACE

Newspaper reporting is a multilingual exercise. Traveling to the scene of the story via a maze of airport functionaries, cab drivers, fast food pass-throughs and hotel clerks presents a communication challenge of no small magnitude. Rendering what one hears into keystrokes that a computer will accept requires an additional language. But for a reporter whose beat is organized religion, yet another translation is required, for church officials employ a vocabulary of their own.

Faith has always defied linguistic precision. But the obfuscation of theology with piety and politics presents a special challenge. Further complicating the reporter's task, today's church leaders often speak of sacred things in sound bites, slipping much of their meaning between the lines. Thus, for those who would report on holy utterance, background is essential to understanding.

On the religious news beat, background involves more than a word search through an ecclesiastical lexicon. To understand what is being said, *deep* background must be probed. Unearthing those communities that have shaped the church's language reveals names that are strange to the modern ear, names like Sozomen and Eusebius, Arius and Athanasius. But listening to the conversations of those ancient individuals is crucial, for they give meaning to our own.

Standing Firm is one reporter's attempt to bring the background forward, to fill gaps that have rendered unintelligible much of what is being said by church leaders today. In this project I have been helped immeasurably by Bonnie Crawford's clerical assistance and documentation, Robert Mills' research and wise counsel, and Kristin Searfoss' design and layout. I am grateful to Whitfield Ayres, Gerrit Dawson, William Hoppe, Robert Howard, Lloyd Lunceford, Warren Reding and Ben Vernon for reviewing my manuscript.

I deeply appreciate the encouragement and support that I have received from my friend W. Robert Stover. And in Patricia Jordan Williamson, the joy of my life and my partner in every undertaking, I have been blessed beyond measure.

– Parker Trevilian Williamson
Easter 1996

INTRODUCTION

OUR STORY

"Our maker, Sophia, we are women made in your image. ... "
That prayer, voiced at a 1993 conference in Minneapolis, Minnesota,
called "Re-Imagining ... God, the Community, the Church," sent
shock waves through churches across the United States. Presbyterians withheld millions of dollars from their national church treasury
when they learned that this conference had received the imprimatur
of their denominational hierarchy. Penalties increased when the
denomination's governing board, the General Assembly Council,
refused to hold its staff accountable or even to admit that the event at
times exceeded the boundaries of Christian faith.

Defenders and critics of the conference locked horns in a nine-
month struggle that many feared would tear the denomination apart.
Denominational officials openly wondered if the organization – having already lost more than one-third of its membership in less than
three decades – could survive the controversy. Critics were accused
of undermining the peace and unity of the Church.

But was it the controversy surrounding the Re-Imagining conference that damaged the Church, or was it the conference itself? Those
who have ruled America's mainline Protestant denominations since
the early 1960s argue that it is the critics who have caused the harm.
Central to their thesis is the post-Enlightenment assumption that
human beings entertain numerous religious affections, none of
which may claim universal validity. The Gospel, in this view, has to
do with building inclusive relationships that embrace all truth claims
as equally valid. Thus, any event that polarizes people is, by definition, an offense to the Gospel and a blow to Church unity.

Evangelicals (those who insist on the necessity of a personal
relationship with Jesus Christ, who alone reconciles humanity to

1

God) say that denominational officials have improperly framed the issues underlying the controversy. Religion, they claim, is essentially a matter of truth, and secondarily a matter of relationships. They remember Jesus' words: "I am the way, the truth and the life. No one comes to the Father but by me." If we cannot affirm that truth, say the evangelicals, then any attempts by ecclesiastical conflict managers to build relationships are futile, for relationships not anchored in God's revelation have more to do with politics than piety, and when put to the test they will not hold.

In the pages that follow we will discover that this polarization between the proponents of faith as relationship and the proponents of faith as truth represents a false dichotomy, for in the Gospel truth and unity are inseparable. The Church has historically affirmed that the Trinity – God the Father, God the Son, and God the Holy Spirit – constitutes that indissoluble relationship that anchors all creation. The centerpiece of this relationship is the Gospel, that irreducible truth that Jesus of Nazareth is the Son of God, of one substance with the Father. In that essential union, truth and relationship are inextricably entwined.

Historically, controversies that have swirled around the meaning and implications of the Gospel, far from damaging the Church, have contributed to its vitality. Like a refiner's fire, intense theological debate has resulted in clarified belief, common vision, and invigorated ministry. In the pages that follow we will revisit an ancient Christian battlefield called Nicaea, in the hope that conflict-weary Christians of our time may gain strength from the struggles of their forebears, and reclaim the faith that emerged from that fourth-century contest.

Part One will recall the Council of Nicaea. Why did a fight among the clergy pique the interest of a Roman Emperor, and what did he do to squelch it? Who were the contestants? What were their arguments? And how was this debate resolved? Woven through this historical narrative will be reflections on controversies that are currently raging in the Presbyterian Church (USA), for the issues that divide us today and the means we employ to assuage them are rooted in ancient soil.

In Part Two we will examine the impact of Nicene theology on the development of modern science, the restoration of human community, the meaning of worship and the arts, and the search for unity among Christians.

In Part Three we will trace the Church's return to ante-Nicene ideas that emerged in Enlightenment philosophy and are currently in vogue among many church leaders.

We will end our discussion in Part Four by identifying signs of hope, developments in the life of the Church that encourage us to believe that the lessons of Nicaea have not been lost, but are, in fact, being rediscovered by lively and growing faith communities.

While illustrations of current theological controversies are drawn from the experience of the Presbyterian Church (USA), the organization whose activities *Presbyterian Layman* reporters have followed for three decades, they apply with equal validity to other "mainline" denominations in the United States, including the Episcopal Church, the United Methodist Church, and the United Church of Christ. The issues facing each of these groups are identical, for although we differ in matters of polity and doctrinal emphasis, we are all beneficiaries of Nicaea and we all face distortions of the truth it proclaimed.

Visiting Nicaea involves more than focusing on one moment in the Christian past, for the issues debated by that Council emerge in every generation. Many religious themes that purport to be new – ideologies promulgated by New Age enthusiasts, eco-theologians, and purveyors of the feminine divine, for example – are merely modern versions of ancient aberrations. Those who know Nicaea have seen them all before. Viewing these ideas at their root and remembering how they were engaged by Christians in other times and places give us a valuable perspective for addressing their current manifestations.

For members of the "communion of the saints," that body of believers called the Church that transcends all time and space, what happened at Nicaea is happening today. This story is our own.

PART ONE

A FIFTY-SIX-YEAR FIGHT

Then it happened, when Ahab saw Elijah, that Ahab said to him, "Is that you, O troubler of Israel?"
And he answered, "I have not troubled Israel, but you and your father's house have, in that you have forsaken the commandments of the Lord and have followed the Baals."

I Kings 18:17-18

If I profess with the loudest voice and clearest exposition every portion of the truth of God except precisely that little point which the world and the devil are at that moment attacking, I am not confessing Christ, however boldly I may be professing Christ. Where the battle rages there the loyalty of the soldier is proved, and to be steady on all the battlefield besides is mere flight and disgrace if he flinches at that point.

Martin Luther

The Emperor Constantine yearned for peace, and he believed the Christian Church could help him procure it. But to his dismay he discovered that the Church was at war with itself. Clerics had squared off over the question "Who is Jesus Christ?" and the imperial peace plan was at risk.

The resulting confluence of faith and politics triggered a fifty-six-year fight.

1

IN SEARCH OF PEACE

"They have also healed the hurt of My people slightly, Saying, 'Peace, peace!' When there is no peace."

Jeremiah 6:14

From a politician's point of view, the fourth-century Church had reason to expect a season of peace. Having endured decades of persecution from an empire determined to obliterate the Christian Church, defenders of the Gospel savored a sweet victory. Constantine had become a Christian, and by imperial fiat his new faith was now an officially recognized religion in the very empire that had once sought to destroy it.

We do not know the Emperor's motive. He attributed his conversion in 312 to a vision on the eve of a battle. In his dream he saw the words "By this conquer" emblazoned on a cross. In the days that followed, Constantine did conquer his foes, and he remembered the envisioned cross as his turning point. God had spoken to him at a moment when life and death hung in the balance. Recognizing his dependence on a power that transcends mortal control, the Emperor paid homage to a sovereignty greater than his own.

Cynical observers see other factors at work in the imperial mind. Under Constantine's predecessors, the empire had undergone enormous expansion. Peoples of every race either fell before the imperial sword or brought tribute to Rome in the hope that such gifts would protect them from its cruelty. But as diverse cultures gathered under the victor's tent, a new challenge appeared. What power could bind people of every race and tongue? What force, other than fear, could inculcate and enforce public tranquility? How does one achieve a sense of community amidst so diverse a collection of peoples?

Could it have been, then, that Constantine, who had proven himself at war, sought a greater victory in peace? His new weapon would have to accomplish what no sword or spear could do. It must be able to unite hearts and minds. It must draw people together, not in fear, but in bonds of affection.[1]

Constantine knew his history. He knew that, far from destroying the Christian faith, Roman persecution had dispersed it. By the early fourth century, Christianity had spread throughout the empire. People of all cultures were drawn into its fold. Thus, the Gospel seemed precisely the power that could unite an empire. Declaring people Christian, simply by virtue of their citizenship, seemed an avenue that would move the empire in the right direction, from force to faith, and from faith to fraternity.

A FRACTURED HEALER

"Not everyone who says to Me, 'Lord, Lord,' shall enter the kingdom of heaven" said Jesus.[2] No one would learn that lesson better than Constantine, who discovered what proponents of civil religion in our own day have learned: that declaring people Christian does not necessarily make them so. The ranks of a now-swelled, officially sanctioned religion encompassed persons – including some appointed to positions of ecclesiastical leadership – who did not believe the Gospel. The fourth-century Church, having survived persecution from without, now suffered a greater threat from within.

How could the Church serve Constantine's purposes as a unifying force if within that very Church there were forces at work that would tear it apart? Unless a solution could be found to the impending plague of Christian disunity, what hope was there for the peace that this Emperor had hoped to procure?

A DIFFERENT KIND OF CONTROVERSY

This is not to say that Christians prior to the fourth century had been spared differences of opinion. In fact, there has never been a time when the Church has been free of controversy. The Gospels record disputes among the disciples that ranged from pettiness (James and John arguing over their relative positions of authority in the Kingdom of God) to abysmal misunderstandings of Jesus Christ and his mission on earth (Peter, James and John's reaction to the transfiguration).

The New Testament describes power struggles (the followers of Apollos versus the followers of Paul), cultural conflicts (the dispute over eating meat that had been offered to idols), and potentially divisive theological questions (the issue of proclaiming a universal rather than a Jewish Gospel).

During the patristic period between the end of the first and the close of the eighth centuries, the Church's leaders had to face scattered skirmishes with the Gnostics. Unable to conquer Christian faith in open debate, this sect attempted to subvert Christianity by applying Christian labels to its neo-Platonic idea that the Absolute (God) could be reached by mystical experience. Decisively defeated during its second-century debates with Christian apologists, the Gnostic heresy has re-emerged during later periods of the Church's history, most recently in current New Age literature and in many of the themes that have been promoted by some who identify with today's so-called spirituality movement.

Although earlier in its history the Church experienced vigorous internal disputes, the controversy Constantine was forced to face was unparalleled either in scope or intensity. This battle cut to the very heart of the Gospel, for the issue was Jesus himself. In what sense could the Church claim that Jesus was the Son of God? How was Jesus related to the Creator of heaven and earth? The fight that fractured Constantine's realm was qualitatively different from earlier skirmishes that had more to do with Church/culture tensions. This one had to do with the very person and work of the Savior.

This controversy was also different from its predecessors in its breadth. Many of the earlier struggles were disputes primarily among clergy in a particular region. Thus, the Church as a whole could cling to a fairly unified corpus of belief, even while some of its leaders engaged in localized controversy. But on the issue of Jesus' relation to God the Father, the entire Eastern Church – laypeople as well as clergy – became involved, and there were signs that the relatively more stable Western sector would soon be affected as well. The near universality of this conflict marked it as Christendom's first major crisis, one that could not be ignored.

ARIUS AND ALEXANDER

At its outset in 318,[3] the focal point of the debate was the refusal of Arius, a popular Eastern church presbyter (an elder in a local church council who served at the pleasure of the bishop who appointed him), to affirm the incarnation of God in the person of Jesus Christ. Inspired by a strong belief in the sovereignty of God and his conviction that only a created being could effect salvation for other creatures, Arius resisted the claim that the Son of God could be of the same essence as the Father. To worship Jesus as divine in the same sense that one worships God is tantamount to idolatry, he argued. Arius believed that the Son of God was Son by virtue of his adoption, not his essence. God adopted Jesus as His son because Jesus responded obediently to God's will, thereby earning divine status. Our salvation, he argued, is achieved by our attachment to this obedient human being who paved the pathway to heaven.[4]

Alexander, Arius' bishop at Alexandria, countered these arguments with a spirited response. "Jesus Christ is Lord," he declared, quoting the New Testament proclamation that had served as a baptismal formula for the early church. He stripped Arius of his position as presbyter and declared his teachings anathema.

But Arius was not to be so quickly dismissed. An immensely popular man, he enjoyed a devoted following, especially from many women in his community and from Egyptian dock workers for whom he wrote sea chanties with religious themes. Arius also found favor with some church authorities, notably Eusebius, the bishop of Nicomedia, who sent letters to church leaders throughout the region defending his friend. The Eusebian letter exacerbated what had been a relatively private dispute between a presbyter and his bishop by carrying the issue into the public arena.

THE DISPUTE GOES PUBLIC

Alexander, his authority having now been publicly challenged by Arius and his friends, dispatched an encyclical letter dated 319 to all the churches. "I wished indeed to consign this disorder to silence, that if possible the evil might be confined to its supporters alone, and not go forth to other districts and contaminate the ears of some of the simple," Alexander wrote.

> But since Eusebius, now in Nicomedia, thinks that
> the affairs of the Church are under his control ...
> daring even to send commendatory letters in all
> directions concerning them ... I felt imperatively
> called on to be silent no longer ... We then, with the
> bishops of Egypt and Libya, being assembled
> together to the number of nearly a hundred, anathe-
> matized Arius for his shameless avowal of these
> heresies, together with all such as have counte-
> nanced them.[5]

Stung by this ecclesiastical rebuke, Arius complained bitterly to his friend Eusebius, and vowed that he would not abandon his cause:

> I want to tell you that the bishop makes great havoc
> of us and persecutes us severely, and is in full sail
> against us: he has driven us out of the city as athe-
> ists, because we do not concur in what he publicly
> preaches ...[6]

Arius' complaint reveals an interesting approach to controversy that has surfaced often in succeeding centuries. His letter does not specify what in his teachings about Christ provoked Alexander's reaction. Instead, he tells Eusebius that Alexander chastised him for disobedience, implying that the issue over which they are divided has to do with ecclesiastical authority, not Christian faith. Arius thus framed the debate around church polity rather than theology.

This same tactic is often employed in contemporary church disputes. An essentially theological complaint is countered with a political or psychological response. Critics of a specified policy or statement of faith are accused of having a political agenda of their own, or of exhibiting passive/aggressive tendencies, or of bearing a grudge for some real or imagined past offense. When this happens, the debate is sidetracked by reference to a subject that has little to do with the substance of the disagreement, and the theological issue is not engaged.

THE BATTLE SPREADS

Together with other presbyters, deacons and even a few bishops, Arius sought regional strongholds for his doctrines. As word of these activities got back to Alexander, the bishop circularized yet another letter, dated 324, warning neighboring bishops that the initially local dispute was moving into their territories:

> Impelled by avarice and ambition knaves are constantly plotting to gain possession of the dioceses that seem greatest ... Be on your guard against such individuals, lest any of them enter your dioceses also, either in person (for the impostors are skilled deceivers), or by false and specious letters ... They tried by running to and fro to reach our fellow ministers who were of one mind with us ... And so it comes about that some people sign their letters and receive them into the Church. I think that the greatest blame rests on our fellow ministers who dare to do this; the apostolic canon does not permit it, and their conduct inflames the diabolical activity of our opponents against Christ.[7]

Alexander's complaint indicates that Arius succeeded in making inroads into the fourth-century Church. Lacking a strong central government, the Church's power was scattered among numerous bishoprics, each of which affirmed its own creeds. Thus, a person whose beliefs were declared anathema in one area might attract supporters in another.

IMPERIAL INTERVENTION

Having been informed of growing division among his churches, and fearful of its implications for the empire's political stability, Constantine decided to intervene. He dispatched his ecclesiastical counselor, Ossius, to bring unity to the rapidly fragmenting dioceses. Ossius sought to fulfill this responsibility while serving as president of a Synodical Council in Antioch in the early months of 325.

The Council of Antioch brought together leaders from churches primarily in the Eastern region of the empire. They examined excommunication orders issued by Alexander against Arius and his followers and found them acceptable because of "the blasphemy which they directed against our Saviour."[8]

Members of the Council measured each of Arius' arguments against the teachings of Scripture. Then they issued a statement of faith, spelling out in a very rough form the essence of Scripture's witness regarding the divine nature of Jesus Christ.

This was not a political document. It made no attempt to find a middle way, a compromise that might satisfy both parties to the dispute. Instead, the writers rooted their statement in Scripture and directly applied scriptural themes to specific assertions made by Arius and his followers. So explicit were these assertions that no room was left for Arius' supporters to sign the document. One clearly had to make a choice between Arius and the Council.

Much to the majority's consternation, the Council's statement did not win unanimous approval. Three members of the body, Theodotus, Narcissus, and Eusebius of Caesarea, refused to sign it. After naming the three holdouts in its report to the churches, the Council declared:

> Through their excessive obtuseness and failure to reverence the holy synod, which rejected their views and regarded them with aversion, we all, fellow ministers in the synod, have judged that we should not communicate with them, and that they are not worthy to communicate with us as their faith is foreign to the Catholic Church.[9]

In spite of their harsh words toward the three dissenters, Council members left the door open to welcome their return. They decided to convene another synod in Ancyra later in the year, in the hope that after a cooling down period, Theodotus, Narcissus, and Eusebius of Caesarea might accede to the will of the Council:

> And know this also, that through the great love of the brethren felt by the synod we have given them the great and priestly synod at Ancyra as a place of repentance and recognition of the truth.[10]

Ossius' report to Constantine brought no cheers from the Emperor. A divided opinion, even if the minority numbered only three, would not satisfy his desire to put an end to the controversy that troubled his realm. To make matters worse, word had reached the Emperor that the dispute had begun spreading into the Western sector of the Church. Thus, he decided to enter the fray personally, preempting the meeting that was planned for Ancyra in the hope that an imperial intervention might move the bishops to agreement.

Constantine decided to move the meeting to a more central location in order to attract church leaders from every region in the empire. The time had passed for attempting to put out brush fires in first one place and then another. A universal solution must be found, a definitive declaration that would speak to Christians everywhere.

The Emperor sent forth his summons to all the churches:

> Now because it was agreed formerly that the synod
> of bishops should meet at Ancyra of Galatia, it hath
> seemed to us on many accounts that it would be well
> for a synod to assemble at Nicaea, a city of Bithy-
> nia, both because the bishops from Italy and the rest
> of the countries of Europe are coming, and because
> of the excellent temperature of the air, and in order
> that I may be present as a spectator and participator
> in those things which will be done.[11]

SALVATION BY POLITICS

Constantine's earliest attempt to deal with the crisis suggests that he thought it little more than a personal power struggle between two obstreperous clerics. The Emperor had sent a letter to Alexander and Arius, hand-delivered by his aide Ossius, asking them to call off their dispute in the interest of imperial unity. In essence, he labeled the combatants' differences personal and political – of little interest in the wider scheme of things – and he declared that such matters should be privately settled without disturbing others. After all, bemoaned the politician, when the unity of the entire Roman Empire is at stake, why get exercised over minor personal opinions? The record does not indicate if Constantine knew that these "minor matters" centered on a dispute over the divinity of Jesus Christ.

In a personal letter addressed to Arius and Alexander, Constantine voiced harsh words for both parties to the dispute:

> I understand, then, that the origin of the present controversy is this. When you, Alexander, demanded of the presbyters what opinion they severally maintained respecting ... something connected with an unprofitable question, then you, Arius, inconsiderately insisted on what ought never to have been conceived at all, or if conceived, should have been buried in profound silence. Hence it was that a dissension arose between you, fellowship was withdrawn, and the holy people, rent into diverse parties, no longer preserved the unity of the one body. Now, therefore, do ye both exhibit an equal degree of forbearance, and receive the advice which our fellow-servant righteously gives.[12]

MODERN PARALLELS

Constantine's early reaction to the growing controversy was that of a politician rather than a theologian. At this stage, the Emperor appeared unaware of the substance of the controversy. Instead, he treated it as a matter of personal disagreement that should be quickly settled behind closed doors.

The Emperor's attempt to frame the dispute in political rather than theological terms found a modern counterpart in the Presbyterian Church (USA)'s 1993-94 Re-Imagining controversy. The altercation arose over a November 1993 conference sponsored, planned, and financed, in part, by the Presbyterian Church (USA) in which Jesus Christ's atonement was denied and the goddess Sophia was worshiped. When alerted to the fact that the *Presbyterian Layman* had disseminated information about what was said at the conference, James Brown, executive director of the PCUSA's General Assembly Council (GAC), retained a public relations agency to help his staff design a strategy for managing denominational reaction. Following that planning session, Brown began making public statements that were remarkably reminiscent of Constantine's approach.

> I'd be less than honest if I didn't say that I'm feeling
> some real anger toward the Lay Committee [pub-
> lisher of the *Presbyterian Layman*] for going to an
> ecumenical conference and then coming back home
> to their home church and attempting to take our
> agenda away from us, by imposing another agenda
> ... I quite honestly believe that part of the strategy,
> if you will, in the approach by the Lay Committee is
> to drive a wedge between staff and elected folks,
> and to get staff way out on a limb ...[13]

Brown's attempt to recast the argument as a political assault
rather than a theological concern was promoted across the denomination by several of its middle governing body executives. Rev.
Verne Singlinger, executive of the Synod of Lincoln Trails, in a letter
to more than 100 regional leaders, wrote

> I can only believe that the conference, and Presby-
> terian participation in it, provided a convenient plat-
> form [for the Presbyterian Lay Committee] to show-
> case pre-existing agendas ... Labeling conference
> participants as heretics or pagans is not only prepos-
> terous, it is a smoke screen intended to conceal
> another agenda.[14]

Another participant in the institutional damage control campaign
was the General Assembly's Advisory Committee on Social Witness
Policy. On February 10, 1994, the committee produced an "Advice
and Counsel Memorandum" to the General Assembly Council, urging a 10-point program of action that included this recommendation:

> Decry the methods used by the Presbyterian Lay
> Committee and Presbyterians for Renewal, which
> serve to: (a) inflame, confuse, and mislead the
> church membership; (b) encourage the impound-
> ment of monies duly contributed for the work of the
> church at the national level; (c) subvert the broad
> mission of the church without regard for decency

and order; (d) deprive members and staff of the church of their rights to fair process and orderly review of their work; (e) create a media challenge to the theological integrity of individuals who are properly subject to the jurisdiction of their own sessions or presbyteries in such matters ...[15]

CONSTANTINE'S ADVICE

Continuing his letter to Arius and Alexander, Constantine took issue, not so much with the substance of their dispute – in fact, he had already declared that the dispute had no substance – but with the fact that by going public they had disturbed the peace in his realm:

> It was wrong in the first instance to propose such questions as these, or to reply to them when propounded. For those points of discussion ... ought certainly to be confined to our own thoughts, and not hastily produced in the popular assemblies, nor unadvisedly entrusted to the ears of the multitude. For of what mental power is each individual as to have power either accurately to comprehend, or adequately to explain subjects so sublime and abstruse in their nature?[16]

Constantine then concluded by imploring the disputants to forgive one another privately in order that the work of the church and – not inconsequentially – the unity of the empire might be re-established without further delay.

> Let therefore both the unguarded question and the inconsiderate answer receive your mutual forgiveness ... for the cause of your difference has not been any of the leading doctrines or precepts of the law, nor has any new heresy respecting the worship of God arisen among you. You are in truth of one and the same judgment: you may therefore well join in communion and fellowship. For as long as you continue to contend about these small and very insignif-

icant questions, I believe it indeed to be not merely unbecoming, but positively evil, that so large a portion of God's people which belongs to your jurisdiction should be thus divided.[17]

THEN AND NOW

This advice likewise found expression in the work of Presbyterian Church conflict managers who tried in vain to organize back room negotiations that might defuse the mounting Re-Imagining God crisis in 1994.

One such attempt was made by Roger Richardson, executive of the Presbytery of Central Florida, who, apparently on his own initiative and with laudable intentions, sought to arrange a private meeting for four invitees: James Brown, executive director of the General Assembly Council, Mary Ann Lundy, Brown's closest associate who had played a pivotal role in planning the Re-Imagining conference and securing Presbyterian Church (USA) funding, Betty Moore, executive director of Presbyterians For Renewal, and Parker Williamson, executive editor of the *Presbyterian Layman*. Alarmed by the denomination's rapid fragmentation, Richardson offered to host the affair at an undisclosed location in central Florida and to provide food and drink for a proposed marathon session in the hope that some agreement could be negotiated that would head off what he believed could be an impending ecclesiastical schism.

Moore and Williamson accepted with the proviso that neither the fact of the meeting nor anything said there would be kept secret. After learning that the two renewal leaders would not agree to secrecy, Brown declined the invitation for himself and Lundy.

A similar experience occurred one year later when, after declaring that key aspects of the Re-Imagining conference exceeded the boundaries of Christian faith, the 1994 General Assembly established a special committee "to seek reconciliation with the Presbyterian Lay Committee." Rev. Robert Bohl, moderator of the General Assembly and co-chairman of the special committee, insisted during special committee meetings that the differences between the Lay Committee and General Assembly leaders were not theological, but political, and he suggested that these differences might best be resolved in closed-door, off-the-record meetings. He further expressed his view that theological discussions were inappropriate to the task of his committee, whose purpose was to seek reconciliation.

Lay Committee representatives responded that they believed reconciliation was only possible where theology was honored as a subject of substance, and that the theology espoused by denominational leaders must be openly and forthrightly discussed. They refused to participate in closed-door negotiations and agreed to enter one private session only when assured publicly by the moderator that the purpose would be limited to discussing personnel issues. [18]

CLARITY IN CONTROVERSY

Many modern church members share Constantine's aversion to controversy. Institutional loyalists avoid it largely out of their concern that it might damage the structure and financial support of their denomination. Many institutional loyalists derive security from being part of the organization. They attend meetings of ecclesiastical governing bodies with regularity and enthusiasm. They love the church's polity. Many ministers in this group have felt that raising money for the denomination, purchasing the denominationally produced curriculum regardless of its quality, and declaring their support for policies promulgated by incumbent national leaders are demonstrations of loyalty and are virtual membership requirements of the institution.

Such persons resent the efforts of those who call attention to theological fault lines in the life of the Church. Even when they agree privately with critics of the leadership – as do many moderates in this group – institutional loyalists express discomfort when critics express their opposition. This "going public," rather than the underlying and unchecked theological schism, is said to introduce controversy into the Church. Of paramount importance for institutional loyalists is preserving the peace and structural unity of the Church.

In Presbyterian circles, a large concentration of privately conservative but publicly neutral institutional loyalists has, for many years, delayed denominational reform. Although many in this group are opposed to the increasingly liberal policies of the denominational bureaucracy, their refusal to challenge publicly this leadership has resulted in their tacit support of a liberal agenda. This de facto alliance between liberal leaders and institutional loyalists constitutes a major reason for the fact that reform movements over the past two decades have been slow to take hold in the Presbyterian Church (USA).[19]

From 1990 to 1993, institutional loyalists expressed some discomfort with policies of national church leaders, but never enough to identify themselves as being in open opposition. During these years, the denomination's slide toward heresy was accomplished in bite-sized increments, many of them so subtle and gradual as to escape popular notice.

But the 1993 Re-Imagining conference produced a crisis that radically altered that equation. The fact that conference themes constituted such a dramatic rejection of traditional Christian faith, combined with the fact that Presbyterian Church (USA) leadership was primarily responsible for the organization and funding of the conference, triggered widespread revulsion across the broad middle of the denomination. That reaction resulted in a shift to the right. It was not a radical shift – for by definition nothing that the middle does is radical – but it generated enough movement to tilt the denominational balance. By the summer of 1994, the de facto leftist/institutional loyalist hegemony had been dealt a crippling blow, one whose consequence in plummeting financial support for the national church leadership has been so dramatic as to appear irreversible.

SOUNDING THE ALARM

In retrospect, even some Re-Imagining conference supporters are saying that the conference was a colossal mistake not so much because its themes were wrong, but because Presbyterians could not assimilate them in so concentrated and public a presentation. However, the conference and the controversy that it engendered actually served the Presbyterian Church (USA) by bringing to light latent ideologies that had been present among members of its national staff for several years. One might liken the Re-Imagining event to the experience of setting off a motion-detector burglar alarm. In order to keep the alarm from sounding each time a tree sways in the wind, an adjustment may be made to the instrument's sensitivity. This can cause a problem, however, because an alarm that has been buffered in this manner can fail to detect the presence of someone moving through its field very gradually.

This has been the case in the Presbyterian Church (USA). From 1990 to 1993 most of the denomination's national staff members who conceived of the conference and planned its themes were at work at the Presbyterian Center in Louisville. It would be the height of folly to assume that they only adopted such aberrant theology on the first day of the conference. Nor is there any reason to assume that when the conference was adjourned and public outrage waned, any of the eighteen Presbyterian staff members who participated in the event and returned to their jobs at national headquarters (one additional participant left her position under fire in the post-conference controversy) altered their commitment to the Re-Imagining ideology. Some Re-Imagining conference supporters simply believe that in this event they moved too fast.

QUASHING CONTROVERSY

Some modern church leaders have an aversion to open debate that runs even deeper than the institutional loyalists' fear of structural damage. Key members of the liberal establishment oppose controversy as a matter of principle, taking their cues from post-Enlightenment relativism, which denies the existence of absolute truth. For people who hold such notions, theological and moral tolerance is an all-encompassing virtue while controversy is seen as a polarizing force that undermines it. Thus conflict management skills command a high priority on national church staffs.

Because they have controlled national church programs and have had a powerful influence on program planning for middle governing bureaucracies as well, liberals have produced windfall consultation fees for ecclesiastical psychologists and sociologists who profess proficiency in conflict management techniques. In fact, a demonstrated proficiency in this field often heads the qualification list in national church job opportunity announcements.

This propensity of national church leaders to avoid controversy at all costs was amusingly apparent in a meeting between renewal organization leaders and three members of the Presbyterian Church (USA) national staff in Chicago in March 1994. The purpose of the meeting was to plan an event during which leaders of Presbyterian renewal groups could discuss with members of the national staff issues that have caused estrangement between the staff and the people of the denomination.

James Brown, Clifton Kirkpatrick, and Eunice Poethig, representing the national staff, insisted that any meeting with renewal group leaders include small group sessions in which "personal faith stories" would be shared. Renewal group leaders responded that while they were happy to spend some of the group's time sharing faith experiences, they also wanted to discuss specific staff policies and activities that have caused dissension in the denomination.

"That sounds very confrontational," replied Eunice Poethig. "I would be uncomfortable with that."

Terry Schlossberg, executive director of Presbyterians Pro Life, replied that in her opinion there could be no reconciliation with national church leaders that did not include honest confrontation between conflicting points of view. "Eunice, you can be honest with your criticisms of me," she said. "You don't have to worry about my sensitivities ... about hurting my feelings. I can take it."

"But I feel a need for you to be sensitive to my need to be sensitive to your feelings," replied Poethig.

Poethig's comment typifies the approach that many Presbyterian Church (USA) administrators have taken to issues they deem potentially controversial. Enormous efforts are exerted to establish "sensitivity protocols" – rules of engagement that actually prevent honest confrontation and theologically substantive dialogue from occurring. Debate must be avoided, for the underlying assumption in debate is that distinctly different positions exist, some of which may be right and others wrong. Debate clarifies differences. It constructs a civilized arena in which proponents of each position may argue their case. Rules are applied to keep the playing field level and to identify arguments made by each party.

Debate that is not content with limiting itself to issues of political process is incompatible with the modernist assumption that there is no truth, only perceptions. For post-Enlightenment thinkers, all ideas are essentially feelings: private proclivities. Persons who engage in discussion are simply sharing their feelings with one another, and, since one's feelings are personal, those who engage in such discussions are instructed to do so with great sensitivity.

It is deemed insensitive to say that another person's ideas are wrong. Thus, participants in national church forums are encouraged to preface their remarks with "I feel that ..." or "In my opinion ..." or "From my perspective ..." In lieu of talking about the objective content of Christian faith, they are instructed to share their subjective "faith journeys, faith stories, faith experiences, or faith perspectives." Using this technique, persons who take mutually exclusive positions can co-exist without friction, for neither position is allowed to challenge the other.

In the light of these experiences with conflict management, we note that Constantine's entreaties to Arius and Alexander that they paper over their differences strike a distinctly familiar ring. Again we hear Constantine say

> You may therefore well join in communion and fellowship. For as long as you continue to contend about these small and very insignificant questions, I believe it indeed to be not merely unbecoming, but positively evil, that so large a portion of God's people which belongs to your jurisdiction should be thus divided.[20]

AFFIRMING AUTHORITY

Constantine's misguided attempts at peacemaking failed. Both Arius and Alexander correctly understood their positions as neither mere political opinions nor matters of private feeling. They rightly understood what their Emperor was soon to learn, that their conflict went straight to the heart of Christian faith by asking the question, Who is Jesus Christ? They knew that there could be no government-imposed blending of their positions, for essential tenets of the Christian faith are not amenable to political compromise.

His call for a moratorium having fallen on deaf ears, the Emperor watched with alarm as a major christological controversy spread rapidly across his realm. Like armies preparing for battle, various bishoprics vied with one another to forge alliances. Constantine's empire was coming apart at the seams. Regional councils like the Council of Antioch were impotent to prevent the impending crisis, for none had authority to speak to the Church as a whole.

What was needed, the Emperor concluded, was an ecumenical council whose impact would be felt in every region, a council that would speak not only for the church, but for the state as well. Such a meeting would need to carry the stamp of imperial authority. Once and for all, the issues would be joined and a decision with universal application would be reached.

ESTABLISHING FAITH'S BOUNDARIES – THE ECUMENICAL CREED

The resulting Council of Nicaea signaled a major shift in the life of the early Church. Christianity's earliest creeds were primarily local affirmations, employed in connection with baptismal rites. Easter day was often the day of choice for baptizing new converts into the church. During Lent, converts were instructed in the church's faith, preparing them for the moment in which they would stand before the Christian community and make a public declaration. Churchwide creeds (derived from the Latin word *credo*, which means "I believe") emerged as a part of this process.

J.N.D. Kelly writes

> Prior to the beginning of the fourth century all creeds and summaries of faith were local in character. It was taken for granted, of course, that they enshrined the universally accepted Catholic faith, handed down from the Apostles. But they owed their immediate authority, no less than their individual stamp, to the liturgy of the local church in which they had emerged.[21]

At Nicaea a new function for the creed came into being. Nicaea produced the first of the ecumenical creeds, documents whose origin and purpose went well beyond those of their localized predecessors. These were statements forged by representatives of the whole Church, and as such, they carried great authority. They were the voice of the Church for the Church, a voice necessitated by the onset of controversy.

Thus, in addition to its liturgical function, the creed assumed a regulatory function. It defined for all Christians the boundaries of Christian faith. Speaking of this emerging role, Kelly writes

In the new type of creed the motive of testing orthodoxy was primary. The creeds were deliberately
framed with this object in view ... The creed of
Nicaea was the first formula to be published by an
ecumenical synod. Consequently, it was the first
which could claim universal authority in a legal
sense. Its anathemas excommunicating, in the name
of the Catholic Church, those who dissented from its
definitions, sounded a new note in the history of the
Church as an institution.[22]

HELP FROM THE HERETIC

Church historian Kenneth Scott Latourette writes that the early
ecumenical councils, more often than not, were characterized by bit-
terness and recrimination that sharpened conflicting positions. But
Latourette suggests that in performing this function, Nicaea and the
creeds that followed it served the Church well. He argues that creeds
like Nicaea identified the issues, clarified Christian thinking, and
enabled the majority to reach a common mind. "In this paradox,"
observes the church historian, "is seen something of the nature of the
Church as it has actually operated in history."[23]

Modern church leaders' penchant for tolerance leads them to
dismiss the anathemas and rejections pronounced by the Church in
earlier ages as "witch hunts" and primitive exercises in heretic bash-
ing. In so doing, however, they ignore the positive contribution made
by those negative pronouncements. Often it is in stating the negative
side of a proposition that we gain a clearer view of its positive affirmation. The negative statement sharpens edges, identifies distinc-
tions, excises that which is nebulous, and leaves us in a much better
position to articulate what we actually believe.

Physicist/theologian John Polkinghorne comments:

Much theological thought has been provoked as a
response to what is found to be unsatisfactory. The
Chalcedonian definition is concerned with fencing off
the unacceptable from the acceptable; it is more successful in rejecting the Christologically heretical than
in articulating the Christologically orthodox. Langdon

> Gilkey says that 'Usually it takes the heretic to create
> the theologian – a fact which professional theologians
> should remember with more gratitude than is their
> wont.' He goes on to say, 'To understand a doctrine,
> therefore, we must first of all understand what it
> denies, and then seek to understand the deep positive
> affirmation that it hopes to preserve.'[24]

Ben Patterson, dean of the chapel at Hope College in Holland, Michigan, writes of a congregation whose new pastor led it into serious theological error. Patterson says he was amazed that this could happen in light of the fact that for three decades the church's former pastor had preached a solid biblical message. A friend who knew the church well described a fatal omission in the former pastor's preaching: "He told them the truth all those years. What he didn't tell them was what wasn't the truth." Reflecting on that analysis, Patterson says, "He said the yes, but he never said the no, and because he didn't, his people never really heard the yes." [25]

Looking to Nicaea, we witness a Church fight that raged for a half century.[26] At times the battle was brutal. Some clergy lost their jobs. Others were branded as heretics and thrown out of the Church entirely. Some were banished by imperial authority. Many Christians must have wondered if Christendom could survive the controversy. But the early Church did more than survive its theological disputes. It grew through them, producing in the end a statement of faith that framed the Church's witness to the world for centuries to come.

Historians who examine that period today agree that the intensity of the debate – and the determination of participants not to abandon painful conflict in search of easy compromise – helped the Church shape and form its identity. Had the fourth-century Church settled for Constantine's early conflict management artifice – an approach currently in vogue in many denominational circles – the history of Christianity could have taken a very different turn. Unlike any other institution, the Church is defined by what it believes. Traveling that difficult road from Nicaea to the confirmation of its creed in Constantinople fifty-six years later, our forebears struggled with the very essence of what it means to claim the name Christian. We are their beneficiaries.

NOTES

1. A half-century later, the Christian theologian St. Augustine would spell out this concept in his *City of God*. Augustine suggested that the source of community is found in a people's common object of affection. He argued that love for Jesus Christ draws Christians together with fellow believers, regardless of their ethnic or cultural differences. Augustine's point may be expressed graphically. Starting from the rim of a circle, people move toward the center, Jesus Christ, and discover that as they approach him they also approach one another. Had they sought unity by negotiating their relative positions on the outer rim, they would have found that in drawing toward some, they widened their distance from others.
2. Matthew 7:21.
3. According to the historian Socrates, the first public debate between Arius and Alexander occurred in this year, sparking the outbreak of the Arian Controversy. Cf. J. Stevenson, ed., *A New Eusebius: Documents Illustrating the History of the Church To AD 337*, (London: Cambridge University Press, rev. ed., 1987), p. 321.
4. The positions argued by Arius and Alexander are only briefly summarized here. Their arguments and those of their supporters are covered more fully in Chapters 3 and 4.
5. Stevenson, *A New Eusebius*, p. 322.
6. Ibid., p. 325.
7. Ibid., p. 328.
8. Ibid., p. 335.
9. Ibid., p. 336.
10. Ibid., p. 336.
11. Ibid., p. 338.
12. Ibid., p. 333.
13. *Presbyterian Outlook*, January 17, 1994, p. 5.
14. *Presbyterian Layman*, March/April, 1994, p. 18.
15. Advice and Counsel Memorandum, February 10, 1994.
16. Stevenson, *A New Eusebius*, p. 328.
17. Ibid., pp. 333-334. One may assume that at this point Constan-

tine does not comprehend the essential nature of the dispute that has arisen between Arius and Alexander, for certainly he would not have placed the divinity of Jesus Christ in the category of "small and very insignificant questions." Later, as we will see, he condemns Arianism and banishes its proponents. But at this stage he sees the matter as a problem of order, not theology.

18. The language difference between Lay Committee representatives and those of the General Assembly Council became clear in the joint committee's first meeting. Believing that a common statement of faith would provide a solid foundation for reconciliation discussions, Lay Committee members brought a three-paragraph, Trinitarian statement (based on the Nicene Creed) to the table. They said that in a preliminary meeting they had come up with the statement as a testimony to their faith, and they asked if representatives of the General Assembly Council would join them in affirming it.

The proposal was rejected immediately. When Lay Committee representatives asked why their colleagues were unwilling to consider developing and committing themselves to a common statement of faith, they were told that such an exercise could be divisive and would be irrelevant to the group's assigned task of achieving reconciliation.

Representatives of the Lay Committee refer to the discussion held at that initial meeting as a key to understanding the breakdown that ultimately occurred between the two groups. Each group had its own understanding of the word reconciliation. Lay Committee representatives understood reconciliation as God's gift of peace to those who find unity in the truth of the Gospel. Representatives of the General Assembly Council defined it in political terms, a negotiated agreement forged by groups that operate from different perspectives.

19. Harry Hassall, a strategist for Presbyterians For Renewal with expertise in church polity issues, has developed a statistical analysis based primarily on data produced from surveys conducted by the Presbyterian Church (USA) Department of Research Services. Hassall estimates that the 2.7 million-member denomination can be segmented into the following groups: (1) 1.1 million evangelicals; (2) .3 million liberals – this category includes

most specialized (non-parish) ministers, and it is disproportionately represented in denominational offices at national and
regional levels; (3) 1.3 million "persuadable Presbyterians" –
people who give little thought to theological issues, tend to see
the church in institutional terms, and are loyal to whoever occupies its leadership positions. Presumably, persons in category (3)
would be just as loyal to persons in category (1) if they held official positions in the bureaucracy. For category (3) incumbency,
rather than theology, matters.

20. Stevenson, *A New Eusebius*, p. 334.
21. J.N.D. Kelly, *Early Christian Creeds* Third Edition (London:
Longman Group UK Limited, 1971), p. 205.
22. Ibid., p. 206.
23. Kenneth Scott Latourette, *A History of Christianity* (New York:
Harper & Row, 1953), p. 159.
24. John Polkinghorne, *The Faith of a Physicist* (Princeton: Princeton University Press, 1994), p. 39.
25. Ben Patterson, "Heart & Soul" *Leadership Journal* (16/2, Spring
1995), p. 138.
26. Although the Council of Nicaea produced a definitive creedal
statement in 325, it did not win immediate and universal acceptance from the Church. In fact, the battle raged for another 56
years until the issue was decided at the Council of Constantinople in 381. One can argue, however, that the Nicene debate has
never been put fully to rest, for forms of the Arian heresy have
reappeared in every age, most notably in our own.

2

ARIUS

Heresy often wears a pretty face. Those who describe Arius and his followers as ogres do us a disservice. Here was a bright, energetic, attractive fellow, the kind of citizen whom any Rotary Club would welcome. Singing sea chanties in dockside pubs and teaching Bible stories to the Wednesday night faithful, this was an immensely popular man. His story reminds us that heresy does not bludgeon us into belief. We are seduced.

History has preserved few original documents from the hand of Arius. Other than some letters and a few scattered fragments of his *Thalia,*[1] most of what we know about Arius' teachings comes to us secondhand, much of it from the reports of those who opposed him. When one considers the disputatious, polemical character of fourth-century authorship, that presents us with a problem. Highly argumentative, these writers did not consider objectivity a virtue. They displayed their opponents' arguments in the worst possible light, and it was not uncommon for them actually to distort what their enemies had to say. Thus when reading what chroniclers of the period say about the Arians – Socrates, Sozomen, Eusebius of Caesarea, or Athanasius, for example – one must take care to separate opinion from fact.

This is not an impossible task, however, for sufficient fragments of Arius' writings exist to give us the chief tenets of his argument. One is also helped by his consistency, for Arian thought is very logical. Once the premises are established, the argument flows in a necessary and unerring direction. It would have been difficult for one of Arius' enemies to fabricate a position in his name, since its inconsistency with Arius' known teachings would be obvious. Thus, although it is arguable whether Arius uttered the precise words that, for example, Athanasius reported in his account of the Nicene debates, the alleged quotes could not have been very far off the mark.

Additional help is gained by placing the testimony of Arius' allies, Eusebius of Nicomedia and Asterius the Sophist, for example, alongside opponents' reports of his teachings. Where Arius' friends believe that his opponents have distorted his views – Eusebius of Nicomedia believed this of Alexander during the early stages of the controversy – they say so.[2]

The writings of the historian Eusebius of Caesarea are also helpful as a corrective to opponents' descriptions of the Arian position because Eusebius had strong Arian tendencies. Although he lacked the courage to stand with Arius at Nicaea, he bent over backwards to present Arianism in a positive light. After Nicaea, Eusebius' true colors surfaced when he joined the Arians in their attempt to depose Athanasius and secure leadership positions for persons committed to the Arian cause.

ONE GOD, THE SOVEREIGN

Arius believed in the absolute sovereignty of God, the transcendent One, for whom there has never been, nor can there ever be, any competition. God is complete in every way. He preceded all that exists and is dependent on nothing. God always was and always will be. When one says "God," one has said all that there is to say, for nothing else shares his being. God alone is God.

> We acknowledge One God, alone Ingenerate, alone Everlasting, alone Unbegun, alone True, alone having Immortality, alone Wise, alone Good, alone Sovereign ... who begat an Only-begotten Son before eternal times ...[3]

This strong faith in the sovereignty of God was exceedingly popular among fourth-century Christians who were surrounded by a culture that worshiped multiple deities. Only a few years before the Nicene controversy erupted, Constantine's predecessors declared themselves divine and required Christians to worship them. Vicious persecution greeted any Christian who made the kind of affirmation that Arius now so strongly affirmed. Remembering the testimony of their family and friends, and the martyrdom they incurred for making such statements, Christians applauded Arius' insistence on one God, the Sovereign, with grateful enthusiasm.

But Arius went further. If God alone is God, and if God cannot be divided, then no one else can be accorded divine status. No other being can participate in God's substance without diminishing God. Arius believed that to declare otherwise is to commit one of two grievous sins: polytheism (worshiping multiple gods) or idolatry (worshiping a creature as if it were God). Everything that is not God, argued Arius, is a creature. All creatures are utterly dependent on God for the fact that they exist.

THE SON OF GOD

Where, then, does that leave the Son of God? The Son is no exception, insisted Arius. God created the Son. Then the Son, acting as God's agent, created everything else. The Son, who became incarnate in Jesus of Nazareth, is a subordinate being. He is greater than any other creature, but he is a creature nonetheless. The Son had a beginning, just like all creatures had a beginning. Thus, to say, as did orthodox Christianity, that the Son always existed, co-eternal with the Father, was intolerable. One would be forced to worship two deities, the Father and the Son, and this would be unacceptable.

Early Church historian Sozomen reports Arius' argument:

> A most expert logician (for he is said to have been
> not without proficiency even in such studies) he
> plunged headlong into absurd arguments, and had
> the audacity to preach in church what no one before
> him had ever suggested, namely, that the Son of God
> has come into existence 'out of the non-existent'
> and that 'there was when he was not', that as pos-

sessing free will he was capable of virtue or of vice,
and that he was created and made, and he gave voice
to many other similar assertions which one professing such views might utter.[4]

Arius, a popular songwriter among Alexandria's dockside pubs,
established his theme in the minds of his audience by repeating the
slogan, "There was when the Son was not."[5] Those words served as
a rallying cry for his supporters, and they became an identifiable target for those who charged him with heresy.

A LIMITED BEING

Logical necessity forced Arius to assert that Jesus Christ was a
limited being, for if the Son is not God, then the Son, like all creatures, is subject to the contingencies experienced by all creation. No
creature can know God, for God is "essentially other." Unable to
participate in that essence, creatures have no means of connection
with God.

In his *Thalia*, Arius emphasized the Son's limitations:

To sum up, God exists ineffable to the Son, for he is
to himself what he is, that is, unutterable, so that
none of the things said ... will the Son know how to
express comprehensively; for it is impossible for
him to explore the Father who exists by himself ...
For clearly, for what has a beginning to encompass
by thought or apprehension the one who is unbegun,
is impossible.[6]

One must even allow that the Son could have sinned, argued
Arius, for changeability is an aspect of creaturely life. Arius did not
say that Jesus had sinned – in fact, he declared with Scripture that
Jesus did not sin – but he had to admit the possibility.

The Arians quoted passages of Scripture that emphasized Jesus'
humanity. If the Son had been of the same essence as the Father, they
asked, why would Jesus have prayed to the Father? Why would he
have sought strength or guidance from the Father? Why would he
have cried to the Father from the cross that he had been forsaken?

Referring to that prayer as recorded in Matthew 26:41, Arius said:

> Nor would he have prayed at all, for being the Word,
> he had needed nothing; but since he is a creature and
> one of the things generated, on account of this he
> said such things and he needed what he did not
> have; for it is proper for creatures to require and ask
> for what they do not have.[7]

SALVATION THROUGH OBEDIENCE

For what purpose, then, did God create a creature with such limitations? Arius believed that he did it in order to introduce into the world a creature who was perfectly obedient to the will of God, and who, in the exercise of that obedience, could then be "promoted" to divine status, a form of salvation that identifies him with God but does not imply equality with God. In creating the perfectly obedient Son, God established a platform, an intermediate, semi-divine level between God and humanity that could bring us closer to communion with God.

Robert Gregg and Dennis Groh see the Son's obedience to God's will as the centerpiece of Arian theology:

> When Arius and his companions spoke of the Christ,
> they thought of a being called into existence by the
> divine will, a creature finite in knowledge and
> morally changeable. By the steady choice of the
> good, this 'certain one' attained the favor which
> God, who foreknew his fidelity, conferred upon him,
> when he 'advanced him as a Son to himself by
> adoption.'[8]

Therein lies a crucial point in Arian theology. God sent his Son into the world as a *representative creature*. Jesus Christ was the perfect human being, obtaining salvation for himself and for all humankind because he represented humankind. Although this creature could have sinned, he chose not to sin, and he continued to follow the will of God all the way to the cross. God's *reward* to Jesus Christ for such a life was resurrection from the dead.

The Arians were challenged to explain Scripture's reference to Jesus as the Son of God. Arius answered that this was an honorary title, God's gracious gift to this Jesus whom God loved. "Even if He is called God, He is not God truly, but by participation in grace," said Arius in a letter reported by his opponent Athanasius. [9]

For Arius, the title Son of God was never meant to express an "essential" or natural relationship between the Father and the Son, but rather an adoptive relationship. Christ was given the title from the beginning – before he actually earned it – because God in his foreknowledge knew that the Son would live a life of obedience. Arius said

> [God] advanced Him as a Son to Himself by adoption. He [the Son] has nothing proper to God in proper subsistence. For He is not equal, no, nor of one essence with Him.[10]

Gregg and Groh, who see as the linchpin of Arian theology its doctrine of salvation rather than its cosmology, conclude

> According to the Arian profession of faith, God's chosen one possessed sonship by virtue of his performance as an obedient creature and by virtue of God's grace, which both anticipated and rewarded his efforts.[11]

GOD'S MANY SONS

One might argue – and in fact Arius' opponents did – that the sonship experienced by Jesus Christ may be experienced by us as well, since there is no essential difference between the Son and any other creature. Arius did not deny this. In fact, he celebrated it. As reported by his opponent Athanasius, he said

> Sharing a single kind of sonship, Christ is one among many brothers. Therefore, as the Son gained his name 'by grace' and was 'by adoption' raised by God to himself, likewise other creatures, being faithful in the manner of that 'certain one' chosen before

time, might be recipients of the Father's favor and glory.[12]

Thus, Jesus Christ was regarded by Arius and his followers as a preeminent human being, an archetypal model of humanity as God intended it to be, a beautiful gift of God, who lived a life of impeccable obedience in order to show us what humanity in its purest form was created to become. God rewarded him by calling him a Son of God, a title that he earned and that can properly be bestowed on us as well, if we follow the pathway that he charted for us by doing the will of God.

HELLENISTIC DUALISM

Although Arius sought to buttress his argument with Scripture verses, his presentation is logical rather than scriptural, an argument based on Greek metaphysics and developed by the force of logical necessity.[13] The doctrinal historian J.N.D. Kelly observes

> The net result of his teaching was to reduce the Son to a demigod; if He infinitely transcended all other creatures, He Himself was no more than a creature in relation to the Father ... In doing so [Arius] was following, despite his consciously Biblical starting-point, a path inevitably traced for him by the Middle Platonist preconceptions he had inherited.[14]

From humanity's earliest records human beings have questioned their place in the universe and their relation to some transcendent reality. Those questions took exquisite intellectual form in the writings of the Greek philosophers, among whom Plato and Aristotle were preeminent teachers. Although individual philosophers developed a variety of systems to envision the structure of their universe, common to all Greek thought was a dualism that separated the material and non-material worlds into two distinct categories. Human beings live in a material world but they are equipped with sufficient imagination to conceive of a non-material, spiritual realm, that, because of their carnality, they cannot know by direct participation.

Plato saw that transcendent realm as authentic reality, the realm of ideals. He understood the sensory world to be illusory, a place of shadows. In his allegory of the cave, Plato illustrated the manner in which he believed human beings become aware of transcendent reality from their perceptions in the sensory world.[15] Trapped in their bodily frame, human beings are not equipped to see reality – looking at it directly, they would be blinded by its brilliance – but their reason tells them that the shadows they can see in their material world would not exist unless there were a light source behind them.

Plato speculated that humans sense the existence of pure light, not only by deducing its existence from the shadows that they can see, but because their pre-material origin was in the light. Humans bear an ingrained memory of a reality that they cannot now experience. Through a rational discipline that Plato called recollection, humans can call forth that subliminal memory and ascend intellectually to the upper limits of their material existence. There they approach, but do not actually reach, the realm of ideals wherein truth, beauty, and the good reside. Although they are material creatures, they can live with an awareness of these ideals, and they can interpret their material life in the light of that awareness.

In the *Phaedo* Plato argued that our ability to make comparative value judgments constitutes evidence of the fact that there is an a priori factor in human knowledge.[16] Since the absolute norms that we use when making comparative judgments are not part of the world of sense perception, Plato argued, humans must have apprehended them in some existence that was prior to our material life. No human being has ever seen a perfect circle, for example, for perfection does not exist in the material realm. But we can rationally conceive of a perfect circle, recalling it from our subliminal memory, and in the light of that ideal, we can recognize that the circles we see are imperfect.

When challenged by a skeptic who says, quite rightly, that we cannot know by direct knowledge that a perfect circle exists, we show the skeptic a lopsided circle, obtain his concession that the circle is flawed, and then ask on what basis he has rendered this judgment. He is forced to admit that although he has never seen a perfect circle, he has a concept of a perfect circle that establishes a benchmark in the light of which he has judged that the sample circle is flawed. The very fact that we render judgments in the human realm, therefore, testifies to the existence of a perfect realm, even though that realm itself is beyond our reach.

Plato never bridged this absolute separation between the two realms. Human perception allows us only to sense the existence of an ideal realm and, by means of a dialectical method, to appropriate some of its universal truths in order to test, interpret and manipulate our world of perceptions. But although we have an innate awareness of the higher realm, we cannot prove its existence, for any analytical tools that are appropriate to the world of our experience would have no application to concepts from the world beyond.

Maintaining the same dualistic assumption, Aristotle approached the problem with an empirical methodology. His careful study and categorization of the natural world led him to observe an apparent chain of causation, which in turn drove him to posit the necessity of a first cause or Unmoved Mover, the unseen, underlying actor behind this chain of movement. We cannot see the prime mover's actions, but we can see, and can even measure, its effects along the chain of causation.[17]

Aristotle's prime mover was certainly no Creator God. In fact, the philosopher did not subscribe to a doctrine of creation at all, preferring to believe that which exists has always existed. But he did see the prime mover as that ultimate force, the *telos*, that activates the chain of causation by drawing all reality toward itself. Although it is not directly involved in every movement from potential to actual, it is the principal cause behind all change.

Moving by a process of analogy, describing a realm that we cannot experience by analogy from our observations in the realm that we do experience, Aristotle concluded that there is a metaphysical basis for material existence.

Greek philosophy, however, proved unable to bridge the gap between material and spiritual realms. Whether by employing reason to examine a realm of ideal forms and probe one's subliminal recollection, or by employing analogy to trace a chain of causes, the Greeks' universal conclusion was that absolute truth lies beyond a great divide that human beings cannot cross.

CHRIST CONFRONTS CULTURE

It was in the midst of this intellectual environment that the early Christians made an audacious claim, namely, that in Jesus of Nazareth, the God whom human beings cannot know has made himself known. Divine revelation has accomplished what human reason cannot. God has come to us in Jesus Christ. That claim, made quite decisively by the Apostles and the New Testament Church, was a major offense to the Greeks. Incarnation violated the cardinal premise of dualism. In the minds of the Greeks, incarnation constituted a self-contradiction.

Although today's church leaders have a penchant to celebrate multicultural pluralism as if it were a recent invention, they are in reality appropriating an ancient world view, for modern pluralism has its roots in Hellenistic dualism. If, as the dualistic hypothesis claims, God is unknowable, then all statements about God become speculative. Theology becomes nothing more than a constellation of human opinions, any one of which is as good as any other. Only the most superficial judgments – a theology's fidelity to the principle of non self-contradiction, for example – can be made.

But there is one notable exception to dualism's toleration of all points of view. It cannot tolerate a challenge to the dualistic hypothesis itself. As long as dualism is assumed, then anything is permitted, the more novel the idea, the better. As Scripture describes the Athenian environment, "For all the Athenians and the foreigners who were there spent their time in nothing else but either to tell or to hear some new thing."[18] The Athenians honored multiple deities, relished their diversity, and nourished an insatiable hunger for novelty. The Athens encountered by Paul would have been considered paradise by modern purveyors of inclusivist passions.

Paul opened his sermon in the Areopagus with the recognition that his audience was composed of "very religious" people. He noted the many shrines and objects of worship that dotted the Athenian landscape, including one "to the unknown god," to include any that might have been missed.[19] On the face of it, this recognition appears to be a compliment, the kind of affirmation that speakers often use when they try to establish a connection with their audience. But as Paul moved to the central affirmation of the Gospel, it became abundantly clear to the Greeks that, far from establishing a connection, he had drawn a line in the sand, a sharp distinction between their gods who dwelt on the other side of a dualistic divide and the God of Abraham, Isaac and Jacob, the God who reached across the great chasm and became incarnate in Jesus Christ. Peter's great confession, "You are the Christ, Son of the living God," drove a stake into dualism's heart, for it proclaimed an essential connection that the Greeks believed was impossible.

THE LIMITS OF TOLERANCE

When Paul declared that God had become incarnate in Jesus of Nazareth and that this Jesus had been crucified and raised from the dead, he lost his audience. The Greeks could handle even the most bizarre speculation about divine beings as long as it was understood that all God-talk was the product of human imagination, the speculation of those who cannot really know the realm of the divine. But it was Christian certainty, the conviction that in Jesus God had crossed the line to become one with humankind, that simply could not be tolerated. From their perspective, this was blatant nonsense.

The particularity of the Gospel has always been a stumbling block to people for whom dualism is a cardinal assumption. Treat Jesus as a great moral teacher, like Gandhi, and Christianity wins universal acclaim. If Jesus is presented as one of the world's sources of wisdom, like Confucius, then he can be happily welcomed inside multiculturalism's big tent. Offer Christianity as the product of a particular culture, and it will enjoy widespread respect.

Keep Christianity philosophical, teach it as a philosophy of life or the product of a particular religious culture, and it gains instant acceptability as an honored part of the modern pantheon. But affirm the incarnation as fact rather than theory, as an event rather than a story, and watch the bonds of tolerance break. It is this particularity that Paul called "the scandal of the Gospel," and that "stumbling block" is no more tolerated in our day than in his.

THE NAME OF JESUS

In America, the first public schools were Christian schools, organized by Protestant churches to ensure that their people could read the Scriptures. The first universities were church institutions, organized to guarantee a steady flow of educated ministers and teachers into positions of community leadership. Harvard and Yale Universities were institutions of the Congregational Church. Princeton was founded by the Presbyterians.

Hospitals and orphanages were church institutions as well. All of these efforts were understood by the Church to be valid extensions of its evangelical ministry, and there was no question but that they would clearly identify their work as a Christian endeavor. All of these good works were done in the name of Jesus.

With the onset, however, of the welfare state, federal, state and local governments replaced churches as the primary sponsors of most of these institutions. Today the poor look to government, not to the church, as the front line for most forms of assistance. Most parents send their children to government (tax supported) schools. Although many hospitals are still privately administered, their major source of payment is Medicare (for the elderly) or Medicaid (for the poor), both of which are government programs whose managers control hospital operations by declaring what services they will reimburse. Homes for children, once called orphanages, continue to be owned by church boards, but most of the children they care for are wards of the state, and the government is the primary income source for these facilities.

In a period of increasing secularization, government agencies in the United States have distanced themselves from church organizations that articulate an expressly Christian message. The original intent of the framers of the United States Constitution to recognize the church as essential to the inculcation and maintenance of public morality, and only to avoid the establishment of particular sectarian groups, was discarded. What was originally seen as the *independence* of church and state was transformed by the United States Supreme Court into the *separation* of church and state.[20] That transition has now moved a step further in the government's promotion of secularism, an ideology that intends the eradication of theism from every activity in which government money is involved. Thus, separation of church and state is now interpreted to mean separation of religious beliefs and values from every aspect of public policy.

One may argue that in pursuing this agenda, the United States government has violated its own Constitution; in particular, the disestablishment clause of the First Amendment. It is one thing to maintain government neutrality among religious groups. It is quite another to promote secularism with government funding, thereby endorsing as a matter of public policy an ideology that has declared itself in competition with religion. To declare, for example, that government funds may not be used to purchase textbooks that make reference to God is to establish a competing ideology, one that claims that there is no God.

Lured by government money, many formerly church-sponsored institutions have sought to distance themselves from their theological heritage. Church colleges, for example, have added non-Christians to their faculties and boards of trustees in an attempt to demonstrate to government agencies (and the purses these agencies administer) that they no longer adhere to the narrow precepts of their founders. Church-sponsored day care centers, nutrition sites, health care ministries, educational institutions, and hospices for the terminally ill, all of which were founded as expressions of Jesus' love, are encouraged to mask their Christian identity by muting their mission statements. They are told that they may identify their activities as expressions of "love," "spirituality," or similar generic attributions without running into trouble, but they must avoid using the name of Jesus, for the particularity of that name can give offense.

Opposition to using the name of Jesus is often voiced on behalf of "inclusiveness." Christians are told that identifying their ministries with Jesus makes them narrow and exclusive. In truth, precisely the opposite is the case. The world has never experienced anything more *inclusive* than that very particular, historical expression of God's love that appeared in the person of Jesus Christ. "For God so loved *the world* that he gave his only begotten Son ..." says Scripture. The Christian witness is not about an ideology. It is not a philosophical system. It is the announcement that a particular person entered the world in order to save its people – all of them.

Lesslie Newbigin, minister in the United Reformed Church (UK) who spent a lifetime working in a non-Christian context as Bishop in the Church of South India, says that Christianity

> ... has always understood that it is not a system of ideas, not even simply a code of conduct, but an announcement of events. Christianity is primarily

news and only secondarily views ... The Christian
can make no exclusive claims for himself, but he
must make an exclusive claim for that act, for the
total fact of Christ, as providing the only point at
which the final issues of human life are exposed and
settled.[21]

Harold Kurtz, executive director of the Presbyterian Frontier
Fellowship, makes a similar observation based on his life's work of
carrying the Gospel to the world's unreached peoples groups:

The mission movement today must understand that
its task is not to invite people to become Christians.
We invite them to know Jesus, to follow Jesus, and
to serve Jesus. We share Jesus and urge people to
walk with him, not to adopt some ideology that may
carry a part of his name.[22]

Jesus, God's exclusive act, demonstrated God's inclusive love in
numerous deeds and teachings. His parable of the Good Samaritan;
his approach to former prostitutes and the woman who was caught in
the act of adultery; his hands-on treatment of people with leprosy
(socially, the ancient equivalent of our modern-day AIDS); and his
acceptance of tax collectors and people from various cultural back-
grounds demonstrate the inclusiveness of God's love. Far from being
narrow and exclusive, when the church identifies a community ministry with Jesus, it declares that activity an expression of love that
knows no boundaries.

By contrast, a community service that avoids Jesus' name leaves
its scope open to any interpretation. How, for example, will a hos-
pice that identifies itself in secular terms decide whom it will serve?
What if the patient's disease is unpopular or if the patient is poor?
Naming Jesus in the mission statement sets one's service criteria at a
level that transcends social, economic, or governmental regulation. It
commits that organization to the most inclusive kind of ministry, one
that excludes neither Jew nor Greek, male nor female, one that
defines the scope of its service in the same way that Jesus did.

THE NARROWNESS OF NOTHINGNESS

Ironically, those who call for generic self-designations, ostensibly in order to avoid being exclusive, often exclude persons who are committed to absolutes, i.e., Christians. In the name of pluralism and multiculturalism, they will not tolerate persons who claim that the statement "Jesus Christ is Lord" is universally true. The secularists' insistence that all points of view are equal is actually a declaration that no point of view is true. Far from an affirmation of neutrality, it is simply a form of the atheists' contention that there is no ultimate truth, or the agnostics' affirmation that if such a truth does exist, human beings cannot know it.

Another charge that is made against Christians by inclusivists is that Christians are arrogant. It is prideful, they argue, for persons who choose to entertain one of many possible perspectives of truth to say that their perspective, and theirs alone, is true.

Only if one grants validity to the inclusivists' underlying dualistic thesis – that there is no truth or that the truth cannot be known – can this accusation hold. If, as they claim, there are only human opinions about God, then one idea must be as good as another. And if this be true, then, of course, anyone who asserts his or her ideas about God as an absolute truth is guilty of arrogance. This was, in fact, one of the major charges brought by Roman authorities against the early Christians, namely, that they were intolerant.

But what if these ideas aren't my ideas? The Christian claim is not based on an idea that some human being thought up. Rather, it is grounded in the historical revelation of God. We speak as witnesses, not as gurus. When we affirm that Jesus is the Christ, Son of the living God, we are witnessing to an event. It is not our opinion that we defend, but God's truth.

When Peter made this great confession, Jesus' response underscored the point that Peter had benefited from revelation rather than reason: "Blessed are you, Simon, Bar-Jonah [Jesus is not congratulating Simon here, but recognizing the fact that Simon has been blessed, that God has bestowed something on him that he could not have achieved by his own efforts], for flesh and blood has not revealed this to you [you did not think this one up, imagine it, or learn it from the scholars], but My Father who is in heaven [our knowledge that Jesus is the Christ is the result of divine revelation].

And I also say to you that you are Peter, and on this rock I will build My church, and the gates of Hades shall not prevail against it [the heart of the Church is the unequivocal affirmation that Jesus is the Son of God, an affirmation whose truth cannot be destroyed, because it is of divine origin]."[23]

Before this truth we stand on level ground with all other human beings. All of us walk in darkness. Every human opinion is flawed when measured against the divine benchmark. We admit with the Apostle Paul that no one is righteous. Humility, not arrogance, is the proper stance for Christians precisely because God alone is the truth and because the truth to which we testify is not of our own making but is the result of God's gracious self-revelation.

What we have to share with the world, therefore, is a gift, not an accomplishment. Thus it would be unseemly for Christians to be haughty about their faith, approaching others with an air of superiority. Rather, we identify ourselves as recipients of a treasure that is meant to be shared rather than hoarded. We carry the Gospel to others, not in a spirit of domination, but in the spirit of love. Having received the truth, we would be most unloving not to share it.

Lesslie Newbigin answered the charge of arrogance as it was made against Christians by Arnold Toynbee:

> Toynbee says that Christianity is defective because by its claim to be an exclusive revelation it has inevitably nurtured the sin of pride ... But pride is not an inevitable concomitant of a belief in the uniqueness of Christianity. If I believe that God really did send his Son into the world to die for me and all men, I am bound to say that that message is incomparable and final ... It means the end of all my pride. It means that I am a debtor with an unpayable debt to pay to my Lord, which he has bidden me discharge by loving my neighbor. There have been proud and intolerant Christians, but the Gospel has surely proved its power to make proud men humble. Pride is not inevitably involved in the attitude of the man who confesses that Christ alone is saviour ...[24]

AN ISSUE OF INTEGRITY

What Paul experienced in Athens was a clash between Christian and non-Christian religions. But at Nicaea, the challenge to Jesus' divinity came not from outside the church, but from within, not from one who denied Christianity, but from one who publicly affirmed it and who held office in the institution that bears Christ's name. Arius of Alexandria recognized that the world needed a savior – someone who could approach God on behalf of separated and sinful humans – and he was willing to identify that savior as Jesus Christ. But Arius was a man of the world, intellectually attuned to Hellenistic culture. For him, the God-man combination affirmed by traditional Christian faith constituted a self-contradiction. Unable to surrender his commitment to the philosophical presuppositions of his age, Arius tried to maintain citizenship in both worlds by creating a Christ who would fit his Hellenistic assumptions.

Bishop Alexander recognized the incompatibility of Arius' faith with that of the Christian tradition and insisted that Arius make a choice. Integrity demands, said Alexander, that either Arius stand by the central affirmation of Christian faith – that Jesus Christ is Lord – or that he apply some other name to his views. To claim the name Christian while denying the essence of Christian belief introduces a fatal incongruity into the life of the Christian community. It was on that basis that Alexander issued the order for Arius' excommunication. In so doing, he was not excluding Arius. He was recognizing that Arius had excluded himself.

This same issue of integrity lay at the heart of evangelical protests in 1993, when representatives of Christian denominations participated in rituals and offered prayers to Sophia at the Re-Imagining conference. Critics of these actions argued that the act of praying to Sophia constitutes a denial of Christian faith, as does the assumption underlying the act of "Re-Imagining God," namely, that God is the product of human imagination. They objected to the fact that persons who claim to be Christian, many of whom were, in fact, employees of Christian churches, participated in the worship of a decidedly non-Christian deity. Witnessing to the truth in a heathen world is one thing; worshiping as the heathens do is quite another.

UNBELIEF AND HERESY – A DISTINCTION

Paul's challenge to the Athenians and Alexander's challenge to Arius suggest an important distinction between unbelief and heresy. Alister McGrath discusses that distinction, citing the work of nineteenth-century theologian Friedrich Schleiermacher. Schleiermacher, according to McGrath, "argued that heresy was that which preserved the appearance of Christianity, yet contradicted its essence."[25] Heresy differs from unbelief, said Schleiermacher, because unbelief denies both essence and appearance.

Schleiermacher says that the distinctive essence of Christianity lies in its claim that human beings are redeemed only in Jesus Christ. Unbelief would constitute the flat denial of that claim. Heresy, on the other hand, would not deny the principle that God redeems us in Jesus Christ, but its understanding of Jesus would be so inadequate as to make it impossible for Jesus, so understood, to accomplish our salvation. Any doctrine that diminishes Jesus' capacity to redeem us, or that diminishes a human being's capacity to appropriate Jesus' redemptive act, would constitute a heresy, even if the person holding that doctrine affirmed the principle that God saves humankind through Jesus Christ. Summarizing Schleiermacher's distinction, McGrath says

> ... to deny that God has redeemed us through Jesus Christ is to deny the most fundamental truth claim which the Christian faith dares to make. The distinction between what is *Christian* and what is not lies in whether this principle is accepted. The distinction between what is *orthodox* and what is *heretical*, however, lies in how this principle, once conceded and accepted, is understood. In other words, heresy is not a form of unbelief; it is something that arises within the context of faith itself.[26]

Thomas Oden defines heresy similarly:

> Heresy is less the assertion of statements directly contrary to faith than the assertion of fragmented pieces of faith in imbalance, so as to lack the cohe-

sion and wholeness of the catholic faith. Heresy is where some legitimate dimension of faith is elevated so asymmetrically and so out of equilibrium as to become a principle of interpretation for all other aspects so as to deny the unity and balance of the ancient ecumenical consensus.[27]

The fourth-century Church labeled Arius' denial of Jesus' divine nature a heresy because, even though he affirmed Jesus as savior, Arius' understanding of Jesus' nature was such that it enervated Jesus' capacity to be our savior. If Jesus is simply a creature, as Arius argued, then he is in the same boat with all other human beings. Since salvation is a divine act, Arius' Jesus would have no power to redeem us.

POSTSCRIPT

In this chapter we have met the attractive Arius, the seducer who would woo us into a most comfortable faith. Arius' Jesus is easy to accept, for he is so human, so much like ourselves. This Jesus we would gladly invite to dinner. We would join him and Arius at a dockside pub. He is the Jesus who appears on the cover of *Time* and *Newsweek*, who warrants a feature in *U.S. News and World Report*. Unencumbered by divinity, he becomes our moral leader, a very good man.

But that is just the point. He is so good that where he goes we cannot follow. He calls us to a perfection that we cannot achieve. Driven by a passion to be like Jesus, to work out our own salvation, we are pitched headlong into the frenzy of works righteousness where enough is never enough. As Jesus "lived out the God in himself," a phrase often employed by today's liberals, we are driven to do the same, and we cannot do it.

Arius seduces us to accept a burden, not a blessing. His Jesus enslaves us. He robs us of our salvation.

NOTES

1. Even the *Thalia* comes to us from the records of Athanasius.
2. J. Stevenson, ed., *A New Eusebius: Documents Illustrating the History of the Church To AD 337* (London: Cambridge University Press, rev. ed., 1987), p. 354.
3. *De Synodis* 16 in Schaff, P., and H.Wace, eds. *The Nicene and Post-Nicene Fathers.* Series II, Vol IV (New York: The Christian Literature Company, 1892), p. 458.
4. Stevenson, *A New Eusebius*, p. 322.
5. Ibid, p. 321.
6. Ibid., p. 331.
7. *Orations Contra Arianos* III, 26 in William Bright, ed., *The Orations of St. Athanasius Against the Arians According to the Benedictine Text* (Oxford: Clarendon Press, 1873), p. 181.
8. Robert C. Gregg and Dennis E. Groh, *Early Arianism: A View of Salvation* (Philadelphia: Fortress Press, 1981), p. 43.
9. *Orations Contra Arianos* I, 6, quoted in J.N.D. Kelly, *Early Christian Doctrines*, Fifth Edition, (London: A&C Black Publishers Ltd., 1977), p. 229.
10. *De Synodis* 15 in Schaff and Wace, *Nicene Fathers*, p. 457.
11. Gregg and Groh, *Early Arianism,* p. 43.
12. *Orations Contra Arianos* I, 5 in Bright, *The Orations*, p. 5.
13. Gregg and Groh argue vigorously against this conclusion. They believe that it was from Scripture, not Greek metaphysics, that Arius came to his view of the nature and purpose of God's Son. The central theme of their book is that soteriology, not cosmology, is the driving force behind Arius' theology. They do not contest, however, that Arius' implicit cosmology comports well with the metaphysics of his day.

    While I will stipulate, as did Athanasius, that Arius made frequent use of Scripture, it is also clear that he badly misused it, forcing anthropological views on Scripture that Scripture itself denies. Thus I am led to the conclusion that Arius' controlling philosophy was not scriptural but metaphysical, reflecting the dualism of the Greeks.

Readers who wish to examine other interpretations of Arian theology will find Rowan Williams' *Arius* (London: Darton, Longman & Todd, Ltd., 1987) most helpful. Williams traces various scholarly treatments of Arian themes from Cave (1683) through Stead (1964) Simonetti (1965) and Pollard (1970). His bibliography provides an excellent list of sources on Arianism that analyze this theology from many perspectives.

14. Kelly, *Early Christian Doctrines*, pp. 230-231.
15. "The Republic, Book Seven" in *The Dialogues of Plato*, Vol. 1. Translated by B. Jowett (New York: Random House, 1920 [Originally 1892]), pp. 773-777.
16. "The Phaedo" in *The Dialogues of Plato*, Vol. 1. Translated by B. Jowett (New York: Random House, 1920 [Originally 1892]). pp. 456-462.
17. "Metaphysics" in *The Basic Works of Aristotle*. ed. Richard McKeon (New York: Random House, 1941), pp. 689-926.
18. Acts 17:21.
19. In fact, all Greek gods were unknown, for it was implicit in the dualistic assumption that spiritual reality was off-limits to human knowledge.
20. Cf. René de Visme Williamson, *Independence and Involvement: A Christian Reorientation to Politics* (Baton Rouge, Louisiana State University Press, 1964). Cf. also Terry Eastland, ed., *Religious Liberty in the Supreme Court: The Cases that Define the Debate Over Church and State* (Washington, D.C.: Ethics and Public Policy Center, 1993).
21. Lesslie Newbigin, *A Faith for This One World?* (New York: Harper & Row, 1961), p. 46.
22. Statement made at a meeting of Renewal Organization leaders, January 27, 1996.
23. Matthew 16:17-18.
24. Newbigin, *A Faith*, p. 42.
25. Alister E. McGrath, *Christian Theology: An Introduction* (Oxford: Blackwell Publishers, 1994), p. 147.
26. Ibid. p. 148.
27. *Requiem*, Thomas C. Oden (Nashville: Abingdon Press, 1995), p. 147.

3

ANSWERING ARIUS

Orthodoxy fights uphill when the heretic comes to town. Adored by the media in search of novelty, a popular Arius can wreak havoc on guardians at the gate. Witty, bright, and delightfully naughty, lesbian "evangelist" Janie Spahr entertains her audiences. How come heretics get all the laughs?

Although the battle was initially an engagement between Arius and Bishop Alexander, Arius' preeminent opponent was Alexander's protégé and successor, Athanasius.[1] With the exception of a letter that he wrote to Alexander of Constantinople and a later Encyclical, we have little original material from Alexander's own hand. But Athanasius, a prolific writer who was Alexander's chief counsel during the Nicene debates, left voluminous accounts of the debates that occurred during this period. It is not unreasonable to assume that the arguments against Arianism that were made by Athanasius later – when he succeeded Alexander as bishop of Alexandria – were, in essence, the arguments used by Alexander with Athanasius at his side during the pre-Nicene and Nicene debates.

THE KEY DIFFERENCE

In Jesus Christ, God is truly and fully present with us. Christ is not a symbol, or a shadow, or a reflection, or a creature, or an instrument of God. Christ is God. That affirmation was the linchpin of Athanasius' theology, and constituted his key difference with Arianism. Arius' critics – as Arius himself was quick to point out – could find no single word in Scripture that expressed that scriptural truth. So they borrowed a well-known word from Greek philosophy, *homoousios* ("of one substance"), to represent their understanding of Scripture's teaching on the essential oneness of God the Father and God the Son. It was that single word around which the debate turned, a word whose edges are so sharp that there could be no room for equivocation.

HOMOOUSIOS: A WORD NOT FOUND IN SCRIPTURE

Homoousios was a term that Alexander and Athanasius had to grow into, for they did not start out with any particular affection for it. At first, Athanasius, who ultimately became its most vociferous defender, was hesitant to use *homoousios,* saying that he would have preferred a word from Scripture itself. He insisted, however, that the term was not of crucial importance, only the scriptural truth that it had been employed to express. Referring to some of his supporters who objected to the *homoousios,* but affirmed its meaning, he said

> ... those, however, who accept everything else that was defined at Nicaea, and doubt only about the *homoousios*, must not be treated as enemies ... but we discuss the matter with them as brothers with brothers, who mean what we mean, and dispute only about the word. For, confessing that the Son is from the essence of the Father ... they are not far from accepting even the phrase *homoousios*.[2]

Responding to opponents who attacked the word as "unscriptural," Athanasius said

> But if ... they pretend as if in ignorance to be alarmed at the phrase *homoousios*, then let them say and hold, in simpler terms and truly, the Son is Son by nature, and anathematize those who say that the Son of God is a creature or a thing made, or of nothing, or that there was once a time when he was not, and that he is mutable and liable to change, and of another *hypostasis*. And so let them escape the

Arian heresy. And we are confident that in sincerely anathematizing these views, they *ipso facto* confess that the Son is of the Father's essence, and *homoousios* with him.[3]

One of Athanasius' strongest answers to the charge that *homoousios* is an unscriptural term is given in *De Decretis*. After listing several Arian phrases that are also not found in Scripture and that, in fact, deny what Scripture teaches, Athanasius asks

Why then, when they have invented on their part unscriptural phrases, for the purposes of irreligion, do they accuse those who are religious in their use of them? For irreligiousness is utterly forbidden, though it be attempted to disguise it with artful expressions and plausible sophisms; but religious-ness is confessed by all to be lawful, even though presented in strange phrases, provided only they are used with a religious view, and a wish to make them the expression of religious thoughts ...[4]

ARIUS' GOD COULD NOT BE THE CREATOR GOD

Athanasius argued that Arius' refusal to accept the essential one-ness of God the Father and God the Son results in a flawed doctrine of creation. Scripture is very clear, said Athanasius, in stating that God created the world and all that is within it. God did this through the Son, the Divine *Logos*, who co-exists eternally with God. One of the passages Athanasius cited was the prologue of the Gospel of John:

In the beginning was the Word [*logos*], and the Word was with God and the Word was God. He was in the beginning with God. All things were made through Him, and without Him nothing was made that was made. ... And the Word became flesh and dwelt among us, and we beheld His glory, the glory as of the only begotten of the Father, full of grace and truth.[5]

The doctrine of creation that appears in this Scripture, said Athanasius, declares that all things are directly dependent on God, not simply related to God through the action of an intermediary. Creation exists as a result of God's intentional action. Thus there is an intimate connection between God and his created order:

> He it is who through his Word made all things small and great, and we may not divide the creation, and say this is the Father's and this is the Son's; but they are of one God who uses his proper Word as a hand, and in him does all things ...[6]

In this key doctrine, Athanasius drew a sharp contrast with Arian themes. Insistent on maintaining distance between God and the created order, Arius was not willing to allow for any connection, even in the act of creation itself. Thus Arius speculated that although God willed creation to appear he did not, by his own action, make it happen. Instead, God created the Son, a being who was less than God but greater than the rest of creation, to perform the act of creation on his behalf. The Son became the necessary buffer between a holy God and his material creation.

What Athanasius rightly saw was that Arius had produced a hierarchy of creation, a multileveled construct that he hoped would preserve the absolute otherness of God. This posed two problems, said Athanasius. In the first place, it meant that God is not, strictly speaking, the Creator. The world is the result of an activity conducted by some being or power that is less than God. At best, in the Arian scheme, God is the idea behind it all.

The second problem, argued Athanasius, was the fact that Arius did not solve his Creator/creature dichotomy by coming up with a semi-divine intermediary called the Son. How, asked Athanasius, can God protect himself from contact with creation by acting through an agent who is himself a creature? Ridiculing Arius for the absurdity of his position, Athanasius asked

> For if it was impossible for things originate [creatures] to bear the hand of God, and you hold the Son to be one of them, how was he also equal to this for-

mation by God alone? And if a mediator became
necessary that things originate might come to be,
and you hold the Son to be originated, then there
must have been some medium before him, for his
creation; and the mediator himself again being a
creature, it follows that he too must have needed
another mediator for his own constitution ... so that
we shall never come to an end.[7]

Insisting on an absolute distinction between God and everything
that is not God, the Arians ruled out any possibility that the world is
God's creation and that God can have anything to do with it. Adding
several gradations of being between God and creation does not solve
the problem, for at some point one must reach the line that, for
Arius, can never be crossed. Locked into the dualism of his time,
Arius simply could not make room in his theology for a Creator
God.

LORD OF CREATION

Colin Gunton, Professor of Systematic Theology at Kings College in London, makes a valuable contribution to current thought on
the relationship that exists between Christ and creation. In his published Didsbury Lectures[7] Gunton demonstrates their inseparable
connection in Scripture. The Bible, he reminds us, is replete with
portrayals of Christ as the Lord of creation, whom wind and wave
obey. Scripture declares that the Son through whom all things were
made has appeared in Jesus Christ to restore the brokenness that separated Creator from creation. "The purpose of the incarnation," he
says, "is to prevent the good creation from failing to achieve its true
destiny: that the Father's intent of love should not fail its purpose."[8]
Gunton says Athanasius affirms the patristic theme that "Jesus Christ
is the Word through whom all things were created, made incarnate to
restore and perfect the creation."[9]

Gunton argues that Scripture does not permit a dualist, exclu-
sively "spiritual" interpretation of salvation.

The reign of God realized in the ministry, death and
resurrection of Jesus does not distinguish as we

sometimes do between spirit and matter. Creation is one, and its redemption does not make that kind of distinction.[10]

Contrary to the Arian view that acknowledges no relationship between God and creation, Gunton says that Scripture refers to creation as a moving, purposeful, dynamic reality whose parts are held in relation by the continuing presence of the risen Christ, the second person of a relational Godhead. "The belief that God has created and is sustaining the order of the world in all its complexities is not a peripheral theme of biblical theology but is plainly the fundamental theme."[11]

CREATION AND THE RESURRECTION

Reflecting on I Corinthians 15, where "death is swallowed up in victory," and "the last enemy that will be destroyed is death," Gunton points out that death is a part of created life and is not negated by the resurrection.

> The death of death that is instituted by the resurrection does not mean the end of dying, but the promise that death will be swallowed up in life. Only God, the one who is both Creator and Redeemer, is able to achieve the redemption of the cosmos signaled by the resurrection. Christ, the agent of that redemption, is therefore inseparable from God the Father in the completion of creation that is called redemption.[12]

Gunton says that in the resurrection, the doctrine that God created ex nihilo, out of nothing, is given its final form. God's creating something out of nothing and his bringing life out of death are parallel activities of the one who is both Creator and Redeemer.

> As the giving of life out of death [the resurrection] demonstrates the power of God over the created order, and becomes the basis of the doctrine of creation out of nothing. As the words of Romans 4:17

make clear: '[he] gives life to the dead and calls into existence the things that do not exist.'[13]

ARIUS' CHRIST COULD NOT SAVE US

Not only did Arius have a flawed doctrine of creation, he also failed to develop a viable doctrine of salvation. Arius and his followers called Christ the Savior. But Athanasius was quick to reveal that what the Arians meant by salvation and what role Christ plays in salvation is very different from that described in Scripture. Alasdair Heron describes the distinction:

> For [Arius] ... the world and human existence are restored through the entering into them of the Word by whom they were first brought into being. This was essentially a minor adjustment within an unchanged cosmic horizon ... For Athanasius, on the other hand, the work of redemption was not merely restoration of the original creation, but brought about something quite new – the comprehensive reconciliation between God and his creation in which through the incarnation of the reality of God himself, created being was given a new grounding and stability in him.[14]

Heron emphasizes the integral connection between the two theologians' understanding of creation and their understanding of redemption. For Arius, creation is, and always has been, separated from God. Salvation, then, means little more than the insertion of a semi-divine link between God and the world, the appearance of a superhuman creature whose special, albeit non-essential, relationship with God purports to offer human beings a closer contact with the divine.

Athanasius, on the other hand, understands that creation, once intimately related to the Creator, a relationship that Arius could not allow in the first place, has suffered a profound separation from God in the fall. Only God can accomplish the restoration, and he does so in the fully human/fully divine person of Jesus Christ.

DIFFERENT KINDS OF SALVATION

In his major polemic, *Contra Arianos*, Athanasius emphasized this distinction between the salvation announced in the biblical witness and the version of salvation offered by Arius:

> Mankind then is perfected in [Jesus] and restored as it was made at the beginning; nay with greater grace. For on rising from the dead we shall no longer fear death, but shall ever reign with Christ in the heavens. And this has been done, since the own Word of God himself, who is from the Father, has put on the flesh and become man. For if, being a creature, he had become man, man would have remained just as he was, not joined to God; for how would a work have been joined to the Creator by a work?[15]

Commenting on the radical difference between Arius' and Athanasius' views of salvation, Heron writes:

> As Arius' diagnosis was more superficial, so his remedy was by comparison trivial: A demi-god, a "divine" power infinitely inferior to God himself, was able to do what was needed. What was this, Athanasius bitingly asked, but to reopen the door to pagan polytheism; to worship a non-God as Saviour, and so to construct a fresh and original form of idolatry. The same Arius who professed such concern to safeguard the infinite transcendence of the One Father proposed nevertheless to worship a creature alongside God![16]

Thomas Torrance points out that throughout the apostolic tradition, in the Epistles as well as the Gospels,

> Jesus is presented to us as acting out of an unbroken oneness between himself and the Father, which is the very ground of his significance. In his miracu-

lous deeds he continues the divine work of creation, and in his forgiveness of sins he exercises a prerogative that belongs to God alone. He and the Father are one in their work of healing and forgiving. That is why Jesus' acts are saving acts, for they are divine acts.[17]

Torrance then assesses the impact on the doctrine of salvation if Arius' Christ had been accepted by the Church:

Separate Jesus Christ from God like that, and the saving essence goes out of the Christian Gospel. The word of forgiveness becomes merely the word of a man, no more than an evanescent linguistic event with no enduring reality, and is something entirely different from the stupendous divine act of undoing sin and recreating human being. A 'forgiveness' of this sort has no divine substance to it, for it is not backed up by the Word and Being of God himself, and lacks any kind of genuine validity, let alone any ultimate validity.[18]

THE ARIAN GOD: A HUMAN CREATION

Arian thought fails on the basis of its own premises. If one starts with the dualistic hypothesis, then it follows that no creature can know anything about God. And if that be true, then anything one says about God can be nothing more than human speculation.

Arius would protest our assertion that his theology results in a God created by the human mind, for he believed in the existence of a transcendent deity whose being is in no way dependent on human thought. But given Arius' presupposition that no direct relationship is possible between God and creatures, how could Arius entertain such a belief about God? How could he know that God exists? Ruling out the possibility of divine revelation, Arius had to depend on whatever his mind deemed to be true. He had no place else to turn.

Athanasius, on the other hand, stood firmly on the premise that what we know about God is made known by God. The Christian faith is rooted in revelation, not in human reason or imagination.

Herein lies the key difference between Arius and Athanasius. It is the difference between philosophy and theology, between starting out in human thought or in divine revelation.

Heron puts it this way:

> God himself must be seen and recognized in Christ: that is the fundamental divide between Arius and Athanasius, and all else flows from that single perception. This and nothing less is what is at stake in the word *homoousios*. Behind the apparent similarities, behind the impression that after all Arius and Athanasius are attempting to express the same faith, lies a chasm that could hardly be wider. The two theologies differ *toto caelo* [literally, 'by the whole sky,' by the greatest possible distance] from each other at every major point; and while they may use the same words – God, Christ, creation, redemption, salvation and so on – they mean quite different things by them.[19]

RE-IMAGINING GOD

At the heart of the 1993 Re-Imagining conference was the Arian assumption that creatures cannot have any direct knowledge of a transcendent God. On that basis conference leaders concluded that anything humans say about God must be the product of their own imagination. The problem, they declared, is that men, who wrote the Scriptures, have forced women to worship an image of God created by males. The solution, they said, is for women to re-imagine God with images from their own experience as women.

In this scheme, creature became Creator, and it was only a small additional step to make creatures responsible for their own salvation. Plenary speaker Rita Nakashima Brock told the audience that God is "not transcendence – that orgy of self-alienation beloved of the fathers – but immanence."[20] We are saved, she suggested, by discovering the God within ourselves.

Brock was joined by Chung Hyun Kyung, who encouraged conference participants to save themselves by liberating themselves from negative ideas like "sin" and by celebrating the fact that the divine lives within us. "If you bring out what is within you, what is within you will save you," she said.

Kwok Pui-Lan told the audience to pay more attention to Confucius, who "emphasized the propensities in human nature for good rather than for evil." Continuing the self-salvation theme, she said, "We Chinese believe there is a genuine possibility for human beings to achieve moral perfection and sainthood."

Conference leader Delores Williams also welcomed new ways of salvation. For Williams, salvation means life, not death, so she has no use for the doctrine of the atonement: "I don't think we need a theory of the atonement at all," she said. "I think Jesus came for life and to show us something about life ... I don't think we need folks hanging on crosses and blood dripping and weird stuff."

POSTSCRIPT

The Re-Imagining event demonstrated dramatically that once one accepts the hypothesis that God and all ideas pertaining to God are unknowable, one is left with any fantasy the mind can conceive. Athanasius warned against this in the early Church debates by insisting that Arius' primary premise was fatally flawed.

We do not create God, Athanasius taught. God created us and revealed himself to us, preeminently in the person of Jesus Christ. Revelation, not human speculation, stands at the core of Christian faith. Thus in discerning the truth of a person's theology, the question is not "Is it novel, or witty, or wise?" Arius and his modern counterparts earn high marks in those categories. The question one must ask is "What is the source of this theology?"

Writing to the Corinthians, who were themselves no strangers to controversy, the Apostle Paul identified his source:

> And I, brethren, when I came to you, did not come with excellence of speech or of wisdom ... For I determined not to know anything among you except Jesus Christ and Him crucified. ... And my speech and my preaching were not with persuasive words of human wisdom, but in demonstration of the Spirit and of power, that your faith should not be in the wisdom of men but in the power of God.[21]

NOTES

1. Background information on Athanasius appears in Chapter 4.
2. *De Synodis* 41 in Schaff, P., and H. Wace, eds., *The Nicene and Post-Nicene Fathers.* Series II, Vol. IV (New York: The Christian Literature Company, 1892), p. 472.
3. *Ad Afros* 9 in Schaff and Wace, *Nicene Fathers*, p. 493.
4. *De Decretis* 18 in Schaff and Wace, *Nicene Fathers*, p. 162.
5. John 1:1-3, 14.
6. *De Decretis* 7 in Schaff and Wace, *Nicene Fathers*, p. 155.
7. *De Decretis* 8 in Schaff and Wace, *Nicene Fathers*, p. 155.
8. Colin E. Gunton, *Christ and Creation* (Grand Rapids: Wm. B. Eerdmans, 1992), p. 80.
9. Ibid.
10. Ibid., p. 18.
11. Ibid., p. 20.
12. Ibid., p. 24.
13. Ibid., p. 30.
14. Alasdair I.C. Heron, "Homoousios with the Father," in *The Incarnation: Ecumenical Studies in the Nicene-Constantinopolitan Creed*, ed. Thomas F. Torrance (Edinburgh: The Handsel Press, 1981), pp. 69-70.
15. *Contra Arianos* II, 67 quoted in Heron, "Homoousios," p. 81.
16. Heron, "Homoousios," p. 70.
17. Thomas F. Torrance, ed., *The Incarnation*: *Ecumenical Studies in the Nicene-Constantinopolitan Creed* (Edinburgh: The Handsel Press, 1981), pp. xiii-xiv.
18. Ibid.
19. Heron, "Homoousios," p. 72.
20. All quotations from speeches made at the Re-Imagining conference are taken from tape recordings authorized by conference officials and sold by a vendor chosen by the planning committee.
21. I Corinthians 2:1-5.

4

THE COUNCIL OF NICAEA

*Like Presbyterians on their way to a General
Assembly meeting, the bishops prepared for battle.
But many had no stomach for it. Putty in the hands
of peacemakers, some were enticed by a nebulous,
one-size-fits-all solution, something so obscure that
it might please everybody. But Athanasius and
Alexander stood their ground. They would not compromise Jesus Christ.*

At the bidding of Emperor Constantine, some three hundred
bishops made their way to Nicaea in the year 325. Determined to put
a stop to the controversy that was now spreading beyond the Eastern
part of the Empire, Constantine had extended his invitation to church
leaders in every part of his realm. The elderly Bishop of Rome was
unable to make the trip, but having learned how the dispute had fractured bishoprics in the East, he recognized the importance of this
meeting and dispatched two presbyters to represent him in its delib-
erations. In addition to official participants, hundreds of clerics,
presbyters and deacons came to observe the proceedings.

This event was without precedent in Christendom. Because the
institutional church at that time was little more than a loose confed-
eration of bishoprics, no cleric could have brought everyone together. Using the enormous prestige and power of his office, Constantine
summoned to one place all the important ecclesiastical leaders of his
day. Nicaea would initiate a different way of thinking about the
Church. From this moment on, Nicaea's participants would enjoy an

expanded appreciation of the breadth and scope of the Church and a deeper sense of its worldwide dimensions. They would struggle – perhaps for the first time since the Council of Jerusalem reported in Acts 15 – to identify essential affirmations that can hold together a culturally diverse communion.

The Emperor himself presided over the great Council. The church historian Eusebius of Caesarea describes the opening scene in his biography of Constantine.[1] He says that after the Emperor had entered "clothed in raiment which glittered as it were with rays of light" and had taken his seat, a bishop who sat next to him on his right rose and delivered the opening oration in his honor. Scholars generally agree that the bishop whom Constantine assigned to that task was the historian Eusebius.

The choice itself was significant. Had Constantine chosen either of the two contending bishops in the assembly, Alexander or Eusebius of Nicomedia (Arius' friend and defender), the tables would have been tilted dramatically at the outset. So for many participants the choice of Eusebius was tantamount to an imperial declaration of neutrality. But while Eusebius of Caesarea's public image may have been that of a mild-mannered, scholarly, peace-loving, and middle-of-the-road historian, people who knew him better, certainly members of Alexander's party, would have had reason for concern over the choice, for Eusebius had made both oral and written statements in preceding years that revealed a distinctly Arian slant.[2]

Ironically, the speech delivered by this historian was not included in any of the histories of the period, so we can only speculate about its content. Phillip Schaff suggests that a clue to its character may be seen in the address later delivered by Eusebius at a celebration honoring the Emperor and from the general tone of his notable work *Life of Constantine*. Schaff speculates, "It was avowedly a panegyric, and undoubtedly as fulsome as it was possible to make it, and his powers in that direction were by no means slight."[3] Schaff's speculation rings true when one considers protocols of the time and Eusebius' apparently close personal relationship with members of Constantine's family.

Following Eusebius' speech, Constantine himself briefly addressed the assembly, speaking in Latin. His words, as reported by Eusebius in his *Life of Constantine*, focused on the perils of internecine strife in the Church, and voiced his ardent longing for peace and unity among the bishops.

As Emperor, Constantine could have imposed a settlement on the bishops from the start, but he wisely avoided that course of action. His approach suggests that he believed a lasting peace must come from decisions made by the bishops themselves, and that the solution must at least appear to rise from their own ranks. Thus, he set the stage for the Council by announcing his expectation that before they left this assembly, a commitment must be reached that would put this controversy to rest.[4]

THE CONTESTANTS

Historian Kenneth Scott Latourette describes what occurred after Constantine's opening address as "violent controversy." He reports that a large majority of participants came to the Council without having committed themselves to a position, but that the two minority groups led by Alexander and Arius were vocal and contentious.[5]

Arius had a spokesman fight the battle on his behalf. Although he had proved himself a popular and persuasive speaker on the Alexandrian waterfront, he was only a defrocked presbyter, and thus could claim no credentials to address this worldwide assembly of bishops. He chose Bishop Eusebius of Nicomedia, his longtime friend and supporter who had carried his cause to sympathetic bishoprics when Alexander excommunicated him.

Alexander may have been more suited to be an ecclesiastical bureaucrat than a master of theological debate. Without question, he was strong in the faith, recognized heresy when he saw it, and was courageous enough to pursue it publicly even when counseled to silence by the Emperor. But at Nicaea he found himself in the company of the most brilliant minds of Christendom. In this arena the case might not be decided on the inherent truth of his position. Nor could he count on the weight of his ecclesiastical authority as he could have at home in Alexandria. This Council could be swayed by a vigorous debater with a finely reasoned and exquisitely articulated argument. Thus, Alexander appointed a brilliant young man named Athanasius to serve as his colleague and strategist for the debates.

Because Athanasius was not a bishop at that time, it is unlikely that he played an active role on the floor of the Council. Presumably, he helped frame the arguments that were voiced by Alexander as the debate ensued. Whatever his role in that particular forum, whether it was as an active spokesman or a behind the scenes partner, there is little question but that it was Athanasius who emerged as the chief opponent of Arianism.[6]

Athanasius (c. 296-373), one of Alexander's deacons, was probably in his twenties at the time of Nicaea. Born of upper-class parents, he had shown an early interest in the Church and had been welcomed by Alexander into his official family. That association gave Athanasius access to the great libraries of Alexandria and an opportunity to converse with the leading theologians of his time. He was educated in the Greek classical tradition. His native intelligence, passion for the Church's faith, and his many opportunities to engage in apologetics honed Athanasius precisely for the task at hand.[7] Shortly after the Nicene debates Alexander died and Athanasius succeeded him as Bishop of Alexandria, where he would be remembered as one of the most brilliant and forceful figures in Christian history.

Athanasius argued the case for the full divinity of Jesus Christ with passion and persistence. The energy he expended in pursuit of his cause, both during the Nicene debates and in their contentious fifty-six-year aftermath, won him a powerhouse reputation and made him the focal point for Arian enmity. Historian Paul Johnson describes Athanasius as "a violent man who regularly flogged his junior clergy and imprisoned or expelled bishops,"[8] but Johnson's basis for that description is not specified. Later in his career, while serving as Bishop of Alexandria, Athanasius was charged with accusations that he used physical punishment against those who opposed his rule, but the charges appear to have been brought by persons who had an announced interest in unseating him, and there is no record of their ever having been proved. It is possible that Athanasius' vigorous oral arguments led to attributions of violence by those whom he defeated, in a manner similar to complaints voiced today by radical feminists in denominational bureaucracies who charge critics of their work with "terrorism" and "spiritual rape."[9]

REPORTS FROM NICAEA

One would assume that the proceedings of such an important Council, called into being by the Emperor and graced by his presence, would have been recorded in great detail. But if minutes were taken, no trace of them remains. Four persons who participated in the Council offer us eyewitness commentaries: Eustathius of Antioch, who, according to J.N.D. Kelly, may even have presided over the debates and made notes, a few fragments of which have survived;[10] Athanasius, who wrote a commentary on the event several years after it occurred in which he included a blow-by-blow account of key portions of the debate; Eusebius of Caesarea, who wrote a letter to the churches under his jurisdiction, in which he explained his apparent shift from the Arian to the Alexandrian position during the debates; and Constantine, who dispatched a letter to the Nicomedians, reporting on the decisions of the Council and calling for their commitment to ecclesiastical peace. None of these sources can be regarded as impartial. However, treated with due regard for the strong opinions of their authors, these records offer valuable insights into the Council proceedings.

THE DEBATE

On completion of his opening speech, Constantine gave permission for the debate to begin. First to step forward were the Arians. "There was when he was not," they said, referring to their belief that Jesus was a creature made by God, a representative of God who did not himself possess solely divine attributes, but was limited as are all human beings. This brought an explosive reaction from Alexander's camp, which argued that the Arian thesis cut the very heart out of the Gospel, reducing it to a mere philosophy among philosophies.

Although no official minutes of the debate exist, we can with some confidence reconstruct the essence of Alexander's reaction to the Arian thesis based on Athanasius' written account of the Council proceedings and the arguments that he employed in subsequent skirmishes. Alexander and Athanasius argued that salvation wholly depends on Jesus Christ being God Incarnate. Denying his divinity would render our salvation impossible, Athanasius said, for salvation can only come from God. He accused Arius of reducing Jesus to the role of teacher and moral example, a far cry from the Jesus described by Scripture as the Word made flesh and the Savior of humankind.

According to Eustathius of Antioch, the Arian proposal was quickly and derisively rejected. Eustathius is anything but temperate in his description of the Council's reaction to Arius' argument:

> The formulary of Eusebius [of Nicomedia] was
> brought forward, which contained undisguised evi-
> dence of his blasphemy. The reading of it before all
> occasioned great grief to the audience on account of
> its divergence from the faith, while it inflicted irre-
> mediable shame on the writer ... the Eusebian gang
> had been clearly convicted, and the impious writing
> had been torn to shreds in the sight of all ...[11]

While it is true that the Arian proposal in its initial form failed to
win majority approval, the account related to us by Eustathius
appears more enthusiastic than credible. Arius entered the Council
meeting with support from several important bishops. He had also
enjoyed a sympathetic reception from Constantine's friend, Eusebius
of Caesarea, and he certainly was popular with the people. With
those initial endorsements, it is highly unlikely that the Council
reacted immediately to the Arian thesis by tearing it to shreds. Obviously, the bishops rejected the Arian statement after it was challenged by Alexander and Athanasius, but probably not as vigorously
as the enthusiastic Eustathius would have us believe.

ALEXANDER OFFERS AN ALTERNATIVE

Athanasius tells us in *De Decretis*, his reconstruction of the
Council debates (written twenty-five to thirty years later), that
Alexander's group first quoted scriptural language to describe the
relationship between God the Father and God the Son.[12] This effort
was frustrated by the fact that many biblical phrases cited by Alexander enjoy a variety of meanings in other contexts. Not unlike modern
revisionists, the Arians seized on this opportunity to show that they
could use the same phrases with contrary interpretations.

When Alexander pointed to Scriptures' reference to the Son as
being "from God," the Arians countered by showing that Scripture
refers to all creatures as being "from God," since God is the source
of all that exists. Therefore, argued the Arians, the scriptural phrase
"from God" suggests that Jesus was a created being, essentially no
different from any other human creature. Athanasius reports:

> But the Fathers ... were forced to express more dis-
> tinctly the sense of the words 'from God.' Accord-
> ingly they wrote 'from the essence of God,' in order
> that 'from God' might not be considered common
> and equal in the Son and in things originate [creat-
> ed], but that all others might be acknowledged as
> creatures, and the Word alone as from the Father. For
> though all things be said to be from God, yet this is
> not in the sense in which the Son is from Him ...[13]

Athanasius reported that the Arians were careful not to contradict Scripture directly. Rather, they employed scriptural terms in
other contexts to undermine their force in the context quoted by
Alexander. Athanasius writes that when Alexander pointed to scriptural references ascribing the "power of God" to Jesus, he caught the
Arians whispering to each other and winking with their eyes. Then
they quoted verses from the Old Testament that used "power" and
"great power" with reference to the caterpillar and the locust.

Commenting on Alexander's problem, J.N.D. Kelly states,

> Whatever turns of phrase were proposed – that the
> Son was "from God", that He was "the true Power
> and Image of the Father", that He was "indivisibly
> in God", etc. – the Arians managed somehow to
> twist them round so as to chime in with their own
> notions.[14]

TWISTING SCRIPTURE

Modern defenders of sexual practices that violate scriptural standards often utilize a technique reminiscent of the Arian practice to
suggest biblical approbation for behavior that is explicitly proscribed
in the Bible. Advocates of homosexual behavior – a practice that
Scripture condemns – have developed fanciful interpretations of biblical themes in order to support their chosen behavior. Louisville
Presbyterian Theological Seminary professor Johanna Bos, for
example, labels homosexuals as "the stranger in our midst." Then
she draws from scriptural admonitions that we "welcome the
stranger" to produce an endorsement of homosexual behavior.[15]

The same kind of treatment is often given to the biblical injunction that Christians love one another. In the aberrant application, loving another person is equated with approving of that person's behavior. Lesbian "evangelist" Janie Spahr makes this argument when protesting the Presbyterian Church (USA)'s refusal to approve of her conduct. At a 1991 General Assembly press conference, Spahr insisted that her being and her sexual activity are inseparably related. Thus, she argued, a rejection of her sexual behavior is tantamount to a rejection of her as a person, and that from a Christian perspective, such rejection is not a loving thing to do.

SEARCHING FOR THE MIDDLE

The Arian and Alexandrian extremes having squared off, Eusebius of Caesarea proposed a middle ground position. He suggested that the Council adopt a Near Eastern creed, historically known as the Creed of Caesarea.

The main body of the creed read:

> We believe in one God, the Father Almighty, maker of all things, visible and invisible, and in one Lord, Jesus Christ, the word of God, God from God, light from light, life from life, the only-begotten Son, first-born of all creatures, begotten of the Father before all ages, by whom also all things were made; who for our salvation was made flesh and dwelt among men; and who suffered and rose again on the third day, and ascended to the Father and shall come again in glory to judge the living and the dead ...[16]

The proposed creed was vague at critical points, leaving room for wide-ranging interpretations. That satisfied the Arians, for they apparently realized that their position was in trouble. They must have known that they could not win an open endorsement of their Christology. Thus, they were willing to pursue a fallback position, namely, to support a statement that was sufficiently vague to allow them room to retain their beliefs while remaining in the Church.

The Arians had no trouble saying with the proposed creed that the Son was one of a kind, or that among creatures, he was "first born." Nor did they contest the claim that he preceded the rest of creation and was, in fact, the agent through whom all created things came to be. All of these attributes could be ascribed to a demigod.

On first reading, the proposed creed pleased many middle-of-the-road bishops whose primary interest was to secure ecclesiastical peace. If Eusebius is to be believed, it pleased the Emperor as well. Writing to his churches at the conclusion of the debate, Eusebius said, "Our most pious Emperor, before any one else, testified that it was most orthodox. He confessed, moreover, that such were his own sentiments; and he advised all present to agree to it ..."[17]

THE EUSEBIAN SOLUTION IN MODERN CHURCH DISPUTES

The Eusebian solution, namely to introduce vague language that is acceptable to persons who hold widely disparate points of view, is a tactic well-known to participants in modern Church disputes. Not uncommonly at Presbyterian Church (USA) General Assemblies, two opposing positions are identified as "extremes." Then a move is made by conflict managers to commit the whole group to a "consensus methodology." The goal of this approach is to produce a statement that all parties to the controversy can affirm. This is interpreted as the "loving thing to do," love being defined as the committee's adoption of a position from which no one feels excluded.

In order to accomplish this goal, group leaders encourage the body to begin their work by setting aside any discussion of the issues and concentrating instead on the group itself. This exercise, usually called "group building," offers a time for participants to get to know and "affirm" one another. The press is excluded, and group members are encouraged to share personal experiences. A premium is placed on relating *painful* experiences, moments in which they felt misunderstood, were made to feel unwelcome, or were abused. These confessions are used to promote group bonding by evoking tears and other expressions of sympathy from participants.

This opening exercise, often requiring many hours of the group's allotted meeting time, is crucial to the success of the consensus methodology, for the intended outcome is the implicit, if not explicit, commitment of group members to "affirm one another" in everything they do. Group members are often instructed to obey sensitivity rules that require them to recast all statements of fact as expressions of private sentiment. In their committee discussions, members of the group are encouraged to be a demonstration of love to the world by speaking with one voice.

By replacing parliamentary debate with consensus methodology, participants minimize the possibility of direct confrontation. Because feelings displace fact, the substantive engagement of ideas is minimized. Facts can be argued, but feelings simply exist. They are not amenable to argument. The idea is not to declare one position right and another wrong, for by definition, that would result in someone's exclusion (an "unloving" thing to do). So all positions are assumed to be valid for those who hold them, and an attempt is made to craft a statement that is sufficiently vague to encompass them all.

The underlying assumption in this approach – masked by sensitivity language and expressions of "love" – is that opinion equals truth, that there are no universal truths, only multiple perspectives expressed as feelings. The moment that assumption is adopted, however unconsciously, theological discourse comes to a screeching halt. All that is left is politics, a procedure by which the group searches for the lowest common denominator at which all members can agree. Failing that, the group will craft a statement that is inclusive of all opinions, even those that may contradict one another.[18]

From the perspective of the Presbyterian Church (USA) national staff, General Assembly adoption of inclusive policy papers is apparently the preferable option for dealing with controversial issues. A paper in which all positions are affirmed leaves staff members free to implement their own preference among the affirmed positions. Thus, for example, the General Assembly's policy paper on abortion contains clauses that affirm both pro-life and pro-choice positions. The national staff, however, has chosen to implement the pro-choice clauses in the paper, pointing to those sections as their "mandate" for channeling funds and personnel into political organizations like the "Religious Coalition for Reproductive Choice" or "Presbyterians Affirming Reproductive Options," and for vigorously opposing any change in the denomination's medical insurance policy that currently underwrites the cost of abortions for any reason (including gender selection) and at any stage of the pregnancy (including late term, partial birth abortions).

HOMOOUSIOS – THE DEFINING WORD

Alexander and his supporters found the proposed creed intolerable for precisely the reasons that had attracted the Arians and, initially, the moderates. To Alexander and Athanasius, generic phrases in the creed allowed too much room for private interpretation, so they insisted on the insertion of specific language that would leave no doubt concerning the divinity of Jesus Christ. Biblical language did not contain the precision that they needed to ward off Arian distortions,[19] so they turned to one Greek word, *homoousios* (substance). If the Council would declare that Jesus Christ was of one substance with the Father, they argued, all controversy over Jesus' divine origin would be settled, and the New Testament's witness to the incarnation would be affirmed.

That argument won Constantine, and it was he who suggested that *homoousios* be added. In a written report to his churches following the Council meeting, Eusebius of Caesarea described Constantine's intervention on behalf of *homoousios*:

> ... he advised all present to agree to it [the proposed creed], and to subscribe to its articles and to assent to them, with the insertion of the single word *homoousios* which, moreover, he interpreted himself saying that the Son is consubstantial not according to bodily affections, and that the Son subsisted from the Father neither according to division nor severance; for the immaterial, and intellectual, and incorporeal nature could not be the subject of any bodily affection, but that it became us to conceive of such things in a divine and ineffable manner.[20]

We do not know what convinced the Emperor to accept the word *homoousios*. He had already demonstrated the fact that he was no theologian, for early on he had missed the significance of the dispute altogether, finding it to be of no consequence. It is possible that he thought – as do many conflict managers today – that words have no intrinsic meaning and that if the mere insertion of a phrase here and there will bring about consensus, that is the thing to do.[21] The Caesarean Creed had already been affirmed by the Arians and by bishops who represented the great middle ground. If the addition of *homoousios* would satisfy Alexander's forces, why not insert it?

THE BALANCE SHIFTS – REPUDIATING ARIANISM

With that crucial amendment, the balance shifted to the Alexandrian side of the debate. Predictably, middle-of-the-road bishops shifted with the imperial endorsement of *homoousios*. That left Arius out in the cold and Alexander in a position of power from which he could press his advantage. With the momentum in their favor, Alexander and Athanasius added other phrases that were logically consistent with *homoousios* and that sharpened the distinction between Arianism and biblical theology.

In place of the earlier creed's "word of God" (*logos*), they inserted "Son of God." In addition to the earlier creed's "begotten of the Father," they added "begotten, not made," clarifying that although Jesus was a human being, there was a substantial difference between him and other creatures. "True God from true God" was substituted for "life from life" to make more explicit the Son's essential connection with the Father. Into the proposed creed's "who for our salvation was made flesh and dwelt among men," Alexander's group inserted, "who for us men and for our salvation *came down* and was made flesh," in order to make it clear that Jesus' origin was divine.

The new version (italics show the additions) then read:

> We believe in one God, the Father Almighty, maker of all things visible and invisible, and in one Lord, Jesus Christ, *the Son* of God, the only-begotten of the Father, *that is, of the substance of the Father*, God from God, light from light, *true God from true God, begotten, not made, of one substance with the Father*, through whom all things came to be, those things that are in heaven and those things that are on earth, who for us men and for our salvation *came down* and was made flesh, and was made man, suffered, rose the third day, ascended into the heavens, and will come to judge the living and the dead ...[22]

Only slightly amended in later years,[23] this statement became the basis of the Nicene Creed that has served the Church as a theological benchmark for many centuries. The language represents a clear repudiation of Arianism. But this statement of belief, in itself, was not enough to satisfy the assembly. In a move that has often been employed by doctrinal assemblies since Nicaea, the Council proceeded to specify the kind of language that would be considered contradictory to its creed. Then it condemned it. This formula of stating a belief affirmatively, then condemning its opposite, has proven an effective, if sometimes harsh, device for obtaining clarity.[24]

In a letter to the churches in Egypt, the Council stated explicitly those doctrines that it would not tolerate. It reported:

> [Arius'] impious opinion should be anathematized with all the phrases and expressions that he has uttered blaspheming the Son of God, i.e., that 'the Son of God sprang from the non-existent,' and that 'there was when he was not'; saying, moreover, that 'the Son of God was possessed of free will, so as to be capable either of vice or virtue'; and calling him a creature and a work. All these sentiments the holy Synod anathematized, having scarcely patience to endure the hearing of such an impious opinion, of such folly and such abominable blasphemies.[25]

THE VICTORY

All but two bishops, Theonas of Marmarica and Secundus of Ptolemais, signed the Nicene Creed. The dissenters, along with Arius himself, were banished to Illyria, east of the Adriatic. Two other bishops, Eusebius of Nicomedia and Theognis of Nicaea signed the creed but refused to sign the anathemas against Arius, arguing that his position had been distorted and misunderstood by the Council. For this refusal they, too, were banished.

What was accomplished at Nicaea would not have pleased today's ecclesiastical politicians. There was no compromise here, but instead a definitive victory by Alexander and his aide Athanasius. What the Council produced was not a malleable Delphic oracle that could mean whatever its readers might wish it to mean. Nor was it a one-size-fits-all document that included a phrase from each person in the room. Instead, Nicaea made an unequivocal, definitive statement of faith that demanded a decision from those who read it.

The Council's decision appears to have been unexpected by Eusebius of Caesarea. His letter reporting the outcome of the debate to his churches is loaded with explanations and excuses for the fact that he voted with the majority, suggesting that before he left for Nicaea he had led his people to expect that his stance would be more in line with Arius.

Apparently, Eusebius had become dependent on his imperial patron. Having been chosen by the Emperor to make the opening speech, he must have assumed that the middle-of-the-road creed that he proposed would receive the imperial blessing. At the moment he proposed it his assumption proved correct, for as we have seen, Constantine did commend it initially to the assembly. But as the debate unfolded, Eusebius proved no match for Athanasius, whose words pierced his fuzzy compromise position. Whether in God's providence it was because Athanasius' argument proved superior, or because it was clear to Constantine that Athanasius would never compromise the substantial oneness of God the Father and God the Son, we do not know, but whatever the reason for Constantine's shift, it left Eusebius in an unstable position. So when the Emperor moved, Eusebius moved, perhaps disingenuously, posturing to his supporters back home that what the Council finally declared was what he had believed all along.

CONVICTION WITHOUT COMPROMISE

It was Alexander and Athanasius' refusal to compromise on an essential biblical truth that led to their victory at Nicaea. Rooted in Scripture, they stood their ground, even at the risk of displeasing an Emperor who was pushing hard for the adoption of a middle way solution. Their clear witness presents a model for evangelical participation in current Church assemblies. Those who would stand firm on scriptural principles today face pressures no less weighty than Alexander and Athanasius experienced. Consensus methodology always calls for accommodation, and individuals who oppose make-room-for-everyone positions are portrayed as radicals. It takes courage to stand against that kind of pressure.

Presbyterians saw these dynamics at work at their 1994 General Assembly in Wichita, Kansas. The presenting issue at that Assembly was the denomination's response to the fact that its national leaders had helped to plan and fund the 1993 Re-Imagining conference. A unity statement was needed, and pressures on the General Assembly to craft a one-size-fits-all document were palpable.

Leaders of the Assembly committee charged with the task of bringing a proposal to the entire body knew that their recommendation must be unanimous, for a minority report would provoke a floor fight in the Assembly. Thus committee leaders cloistered their members and applied heavy doses of consensus methodology. Self-proclaimed moderates wanted to affirm the right of denomination leaders to participate in "ecumenical events" like the Re-Imagining conference, and to have the freedom of theological expression. Other than an admission that some statements at the conference were in "bad taste" there was to be no significant criticism of the event or the theology that its leaders espoused. Pressure from the politically correct toward the adoption of an "inclusivist position" was intense.

One member of that committee distinguished himself in Wichita. Keith Lindstrom, a seminary student whose future ministry opportunities could have been badly damaged had he been judged a right-wing radical, dared to tell the committee that he would not vote for any document that failed to recognize the fact that the Re-Imagining conference had exceeded the boundaries of Christian faith. That declaration was Keith Lindstrom's *homoousios*. He insisted that the committee report declare that inclusivism has its limits, that there are boundaries beyond which one cannot claim the name Christian.

Lindstrom's refusal to give ground on this point won other, more reticent committee members who had privately shared his view but had been unwilling to express it publicly. As a handful of votes moved in Lindstrom's direction committee leaders recognized the looming threat of a minority report. Only by including the language that Lindstrom had specified could this group produce a unanimous recommendation to the Assembly.

Following marathon negotiating sessions during which the seminary student underwent enormous pressure to compromise his stance, the committee unanimously adopted Lindstrom's language, and a grateful General Assembly voted 516-4 to approve its report.

> We reject teachings that deny the tenets of our faith.
> Let there be no doubt that theology matters, that our
> Reformed tradition is precious to us, and that we
> intend to hand it down to the next generation: our
> children and our grandchildren ...[26]

In their action on the report the commissioners affirmed their belief in the triune God, the uniqueness of God's incarnation in Jesus Christ, and the death and resurrection of Jesus Christ for our salvation. They affirmed that the Scriptures, by the Holy Spirit, are the unique and authoritative witness to Jesus Christ, and they reaffirmed their commitment to "the faith once delivered [and] historically expressed in the Nicene and Apostles' Creeds, and the other historic confessions of our church."[27]

Presbyterians hugged one another in the aisles and sang "Amazing Grace." News reports labeled the action "Miracle in Wichita." Renewal organizations within the denomination lauded the decision as a major turning point, a benchmark to which they could hold national church leadership accountable should it again promote syncretism in the name of the Christian Church.

It would be inaccurate to say that one seminary student's conviction became the axis on which the Wichita General Assembly turned. Hundreds of congregations had declared their objections to Re-Imagining. Fifty-one presbyteries representing hundreds of thousands of Presbyterians had sent overtures to the General Assembly. Scores of people testified in Wichita. Although Lindstrom's witness alone did not turn the tide, events there would not have unfolded in the way that they did without his singular contribution.

THE NICENE COUNCIL ADJOURNS

As the bishops made their way back to their territories, they knew something of crucial importance had happened at Nicaea. The Church had issued a definitive declaration of faith. Arius and his two supporters were banished. Athanasius returned to Alexandria a victor, soon to occupy the bishop's chair when Alexander died in 328. And Constantine returned to his throne, believing that the peace he so fervently desired for his empire had finally been won.

NOTES

1. *Vita Constantini,* III, 10 in Schaff, P., and H. Wace, eds., *The Nicene and Post-Nicene Fathers.* Series II, Vol. I (New York: The Christian Literature Company, 1892), p.522.

2. Church historians have vigorously debated the role that Eusebius of Caesarea played in this controversy before, during and after the Council of Nicaea. Eusebius was a staunch opponent of Sabellianism. (This heresy refused to acknowledge the full humanity of Jesus Christ, preferring to believe that Jesus was merely a human form, something like a suit of clothes that was draped over the divine presence, so that God only appeared to be human.) In the course of an argument against Sabellianism, Eusebius wrote a letter to Paulinus of Tyre that suggested his support for Arius' ideas. Later, Arius himself wrote a letter to his friend and lifelong defender, Eusebius of Nicomedia, in which he named Eusebius of Caesarea as one who agreed with some of his fundamental doctrines. Additionally, Eusebius of Caesarea wrote to Alexander during the heat of the controversy, complaining that in his attack on Arius, Alexander had distorted the Arian position. And later, although he voted to adopt the Nicene statement (including its anathemas against Arius), he participated in several attempts to defrock and banish Athanasius, Arius' chief opponent in the Nicene debate. These incidents, in addition to evidence of overt hostility and suspicion held by Athanasius' supporters toward Eusebius of Caesarea, have led some scholars to conclude that Constantine's choice for the opening speech was anything but neutral, and that the table had been tilted toward the Arian side of the debate.

Other scholars, e.g., Philip Schaff and Henry Wace, argue that the evidence cited above can be interpreted differently. They argue that Eusebius' Arian-sounding comments in the years preceding the Council meeting must be read in the light of his debate with Sabellianism. Schaff and others argue that in challenging this heresy, Eusebius may have leaned a little too much toward the opposite extreme (Arianism) in order to emphasize a point, but that, in itself, did not mean that he affirmed Arius' the-

ology. Further, they suggest that in the early stages of the controversy, Eusebius may not have believed that Arius' views were as
radical as they actually turned out to be, so that when the full
dimensions of Arianism became clear during the council debate,
Eusebius voted with the majority and declared his distance from
Arius.

3. Schaff and Wace, *Nicene Fathers*, p. 20.

4. The fact that Constantine chose not to impose a preemptory settlement on the Council does not mean that he chose not to be
   involved. As we shall see, the Emperor played an active role in
   pushing for a solution. But at the outset, he withheld his hand,
   allowing alternatives to arise from the bishops themselves. It was
   apparently only after he could see the drift of the majority during
   the ensuing debates that he re-entered the discussion in favor of
   the prevailing position.

5. Kenneth Scott Latourette, *A History of Christianity* (New York:
   Harper and Row, 1953), p. 154.

6. This speculation gains some credence from the fact that following Alexander's victory at Nicaea, the Arian forces targeted
   Athanasius for retaliation. These developments are discussed in
   more detail in Chapter 5.

7. Cf. Socrates, *Scholasticus Ecclesiastical History* I, 8 in Schaff
   and Wace, *Nicene Fathers,* Series II, Vol. II, p. 9.

8. Paul Johnson, *A History of Christianity* (New York: Simon &
   Schuster, 1976), p. 87.

9. These charges were made against the *Presbyterian Layman* in an
   undated paper prepared for the General Assembly Council by
   Donna Blackstock, Coordinator for Resource Development at
   the Presbyterian Center in Louisville, Kentucky.

10. J.N.D. Kelly, *Early Christian Creeds*, Third Edition, (London:
    Longman Group Limited, 1972), p. 213.

11. Theodoret, *Ecclesiastical History* I, 7 in Schaff and Wace,
    Nicene Fathers, Series II, Vol. III, p. 44.

12. *De Decretis* 19, 20 in Schaff and Wace, *Nicene Fathers,* Series
    II, Vol. IV, pp. 162-163.

13. *De Decretis* 5 in Schaff and Wace, *Nicene Fathers,* p. 162.

14. Kelly, p. 213.

15. Johanna Bos made these comments in testimony before the Commissioners' Committee on Human Sexuality at the 1993 General Assembly in Orlando, Florida, and again at the Indian Nations Presbytery clergy retreat, Oct. 11-13, 1993, where she was the keynote speaker. The same message was promoted at the July 13-18, 1994, Presbyterian Women's Gathering in Ames, Iowa, where a theme was "Welcoming the Stranger."

16. J. Stevenson, ed., *A New Eusebius: Documents Illustrating the History of the Church To AD 337* (London: Cambridge University Press, rev. ed., 1987), p. 345.

17. Ibid., p. 344.

18. Examples of this process abound at each annual General Assembly of the Presbyterian Church (USA). One of the most dramatic instances, however, occurred at the denomination's highly touted Chicago Convocation that met October 29–November 1, 1992. Faced with an impending financial crisis that mandated a radical reduction and restructure of their national offices, General Assembly leaders invited a wildly diverse gathering of 467 Presbyterians to determine what a denomination with limited resources ought to do. A process manager was employed. Committed to an egalitarian ideal, he told members of the group that all of their ideas would be deemed of equal value. Their task was to write these ideas on sheets of newsprint that papered the walls of a huge ballroom. Before you leave this hotel, promised the consultant, each of you will be given a book that contains all of the ideas expressed in this place, your own personal copy of this consultation's product. The resulting book, containing a cacophony of more than 300 proposals, many of which contradicted one another, was given to a planning team as a basis for the new national Church restructure. The first copy extruded by an in-house computer was held aloft as participants sang "Amazing Grace" while hugging one another.

19. Hebrew and Aramaic languages, the languages of the Old Testament and of Jesus of Nazareth, are heavily metaphorical. When employed in Scripture, these words take on a flavor of meaning that arises from the faith culture in which they were passed down orally from generation to generation. When one lifts a word from this context and tries to insert it into the language of another cul-

ture, Hellenistic culture, for example, it is often impossible to find a word-for-word equivalency. Anyone who has studied a language other than his or her native tongue knows that a word in one culture can mean something entirely different in another.

This was part of the problem experienced by Alexander and Athanasius at Nicaea. When they attempted to translate scriptural terms directly into Greek terms, they found that the cultural flavors underlying those words made a one-for-one equivalency impossible. That is why their early attempts to express scriptural truth using scriptural terms in a Hellenistic cultural milieu made them sitting ducks for Hellenists like Arius. Their only choice was to abandon the words explicitly used by Scripture and choose a very different Greek word that more accurately expressed the truth they were trying to convey.

20. Stevenson, *A New Eusebius*, p. 345.

21. The Emperor's waffling, both before and after Nicaea, lends credence to this possibility. What this man wanted, more than anything else, was peace, a goal that is often not well served by linguistic precision.

22. Emphasis added.

23. The Council of Constantinople in 381 added a section strengthening Nicaea's affirmation of the full deity of the Holy Spirit.

24. This device of stating a truth followed by its mirror image has biblical roots. Proverbs 15:1 says: "A soft answer turns away wrath, But a harsh word stirs up anger," or Proverbs 13:4: "The soul of the sluggard desires and has nothing; But the soul of the diligent shall be made rich." Anathemas included in early Church creeds provided a clarifying contrast with their earlier affirmations and accentuated the creed's affirmative declarations. As harsh as they may appear to modern readers, they offer welcome precision to those who suffer from the vagueness of today's feel-good religion.

25. Stevenson, *A New Eusebius,* p. 348.

26. Minutes of the 206th General Assembly (1994), Presbyterian Church (USA), Part I, p. 88.

27. Ibid.

5

PIETY AND POLITICS: THE BATTLE CONTINUES

"It ain't over til it's over." Yogi Berra's wisdom applies to faith as well as baseball. Signing a creed is one thing; inscribing that creed's faith on the heart is another. An imperial pronouncement in Nicaea, like a moderator's gavel in Wichita, declared that the contest was over. But a battle for the soul of the Church rages on.

Constantine's peace declaration was premature. For fifty-six years, until the Council of Constantinople (381), the church found itself embroiled in battles, at times fearsome, over the issue that Nicaea had supposedly put to rest. Some skirmishes were theological, but many more were fought in the arena of power politics.

Alasdair I.C. Heron suggests that the continuing struggle was due partly to the fact that Nicaea did a better job in spelling out what it rejected than in saying what it affirmed. Referring to the Council's use of the term *homoousios*, he says

> [It] was primarily *negative*: it was a means of excluding Arian theology. Its positive meaning was never very clearly explored ... so the word became a subject of bitter controversy for a further half century ... Having spoken at Nicaea, the Church was faced with the task of deciding what it had meant.[1]

SEARCHING FOR ANOTHER WORD

Everyone at Nicaea agreed that *homoousios* was a thorny word. As we saw earlier, even Athanasius was willing to entertain an alternative if one could be found that would accurately reflect Scripture's teaching regarding the person and work of Jesus Christ. During the next half century, regional councils attempted to come up with alternative language.

The Second Creed of Antioch (341) called the Son the "exact image of the Godhead." This option failed to take hold in the Church because it left unclear how the Son according to this definition is substantially different from any other human being. All humans are made in the image of God, and a mere difference in degree does nothing to free the Son from the creature side of dualism's divide.

The Second Creed of Sirmium (357) declared that the Son was "unlike the Father." It emphasized the difference between the origins of the Father and the Son by calling the Father "unbegotten" and the Son "begotten." The creed had a distinctly Arian flavor and did not gain wide approval.

The Fourth Creed of Sirmium (357) said that the Son was "like the Father who begot him according to the Scriptures," and that he was "like the Father in all things." But what does it mean that Jesus was "like the Father," and how does that description account for his uniqueness as the Son of God? Are there others who would qualify as being like the Father, and is it possible that someone else may appear who is more like the Father than Jesus was? If one says that the Son is like the Father, by what benchmark does one make that comparison? These kinds of questions left the Fourth Creed of Sirmium with waning support.

The Council of Ancyra (358) said that the Son was not a creature, but was "of like essence with the Father." This attempt at a middle ground, like the option proposed by the Fourth Creed of Sirmium, had little staying power, for it left the Church wondering how it could claim with Scripture that in Jesus Christ God had done something decisive and final for our salvation. Although it saw the Son as more than a creature, it was unable to say that the Son's essence was identical with the Father. But if the Son is simply of like essence with the Father, doesn't that leave open the possibility that there might be others who would resemble that essence more fully?

And isn't there a world of difference between being of like essence and being of the same essence? In effect, this option makes Christianity merely one of many religious alternatives.

None of these options took hold in the Church because each failed to convey Scripture's cardinal affirmation that in Jesus of Nazareth the world had encountered nothing less than God himself. The Church discovered that any attempt to modify that claim catapults it into the Arian camp, excises the heart of the Gospel, and leaves the world with a saviour who has no power to save. Thus the *homoousios* supporters, while tentative in their commitment to the term early in the controversy, became increasingly supportive of it each time alternatives were considered. The word had to be *homoousios,* they decided. Any modification pales in contrast.

TURNING TO POLITICS

At Nicaea the contestants had argued theology. In its aftermath, with the exception of the occasional regional attempts to find a theological middle ground mentioned above, the struggle increasingly turned to politics. Having been soundly defeated on theological grounds, Arian forces tried to discredit and depose those theologians who had been *homoousios'* ablest defenders.

Thus, Athanasius became the target of vicious, personal and unrelenting attacks. His steadfastness in the face of overwhelming opposition was noted by both religious and secular observers. Even the historian Edward Gibbon, who had little use for Christianity, recognized the force of Athanasius' character throughout the struggle. In his *Rise and Fall of the Roman Empire*, Gibbon described Athanasius as a man whose "superiority of character and abilities ... would have qualified him far better than the degenerate sons of Constantine for the government of a great monarchy."[2] Gibbon considered the bishop a single-minded man of great will power and determination who would not sacrifice his faith, even when challenged by the Emperor himself.

ARIUS RETURNS

The Arians' first step was to have their hero and his supporters returned from exile. In 327 Constantine received a letter from Arius requesting that he be allowed to come home. Arius' letter included a statement of faith that, on its face, appeared orthodox. Contrasted with the opinions he had declared seven years earlier in his letter to Eusebius of Nicomedia, it did exhibit some movement in the Nicene direction. Said Arius:

> We believe in God the Father Almighty and in the Lord Jesus Christ his only begotten Son, who was begotten of him before all ages, God the Word through whom all things were made, both those which are in the heavens and those upon the earth; who descended, and took flesh, and suffered, and rose again, ascended into the heavens, and is coming again to judge the living and dead ...[3]

Although Arius' confession conceded that Jesus "descended and took flesh," he did not say, as had the Council of Nicaea, that the Son was of the same essence with the Father. Athanasius, who understood that what a person will not say can be more important than what he says, noted Arius' omission and publicly opposed his restoration on those grounds. Anxious to quell discord and to satisfy bishops who continued to plead on Arius' behalf, Constantine spurned Athanasius' counsel, acceded to the request, and ended Arius' exile.

MODERN PARALLELS

The modern Church could well pay heed to this incident and its aftermath, for its politics of inclusiveness follows a path not unlike the one that Constantine chose. In an attempt to achieve reconciliation and a united front in dealing with social problems, ecclesiastical politicians often bracket or ignore key theological differences. A recent example of this may be seen in statements of Konrad Raiser, Executive Secretary of the World Council of Churches. Raiser has urged WCC leaders to focus on the fact that their common goal is to change the structures of society, particularly as they relate to economic relationships between developed and underdeveloped countries, and to downplay or ignore theological differences. January 31, 1995, discussions held by ecumenical leaders in Chile included statements that the ecumenical community should broaden its boundaries to include non-Christian faith groups that pursue compatible social goals.

Even the Presbyterian Church (USA), a constitutional church whose members subscribe to a particular faith that is stated in its confessional documents, has had problems in recent years with the blurring of its doctrinal distinctiveness by denominational officials. The General Assembly Council's refusal to declare that its staff members exceeded the boundaries of Christian faith when they worshiped Sophia was defended on grounds that the event in which this worship service occurred was "ecumenical." Criticisms from across the denomination that this use of the word has leeched it of any meaningful connection with its Christian origin have led Presbyterian officials to amend the name of one of their national offices to the Office of Ecumenical *and Interfaith* Relations. Neither the tasks nor the personnel of that office have been significantly changed, only the name. One of the office's most recent efforts has been to develop guidelines for joint participation in worship events with non-Christian religions.

THE COUNCIL OF NICOMEDIA

Constantine's decision to lift Arius' banishment addressed the issue of his location but it was left to the bishops to decide on his standing in the church. In 327, the Emperor met with bishops at the Council of Nicomedia and asked them to examine Arius' confession of faith and take up the issue of his request for restoration to communion. The bishops did so, and found Arius worthy of restoration.

Athanasius was vigorous in his opposition, and declared publicly that he had no intention of admitting Arius and his supporters to communion. That announcement struck Constantine as an affront to imperial authority, and it triggered a hostile reaction. Athanasius reported the incident as follows:

> And when I refused, declaring that it was not right
> that those who had invented heresy contrary to the
> truth and had been anathematized by the Ecumenical Council should be admitted to communion,
> [Eusebius of Caesarea] caused the Emperor also,
> Constantine, of blessed memory, to write to me,

threatening me in case I should not receive Arius and his fellows.[4]

Athanasius quoted a portion of Constantine's threatening letter:

Having therefore knowledge of my will, grant free admission to all who wish to enter into the Church. For if I learn that you have hindered or excluded any who claim to be admitted into communion with the Church, I will immediately send someone who shall depose you by my command, and shall remove you from your place.[5]

The ink had hardly dried on Arius' restoration when Eusebius of Nicomedia, Arius' chief spokesman at Nicaea, requested a similar pardon for himself. Writing to church officials, he said that he had never been a heretic, that he agreed with the creed of Nicaea, and that his only offense was his refusal to sign the Council's anathema against Arius, believing that Arius' position had been misunderstood. Eusebius pleaded:

We subscribed the declaration of faith; we did not subscribe the anathematizing; not as objecting to the creed, but as disbelieving the party accused to be such as was represented, having been satisfied on this point, both from his own letters to us, and from personal conversations ... If therefore you should now think fit to restore us to your presence, you will have us on all points conformable, and acquiescent in your decrees, especially since it has seemed good to your piety to deal tenderly with and recall even him who was primarily accused [Arius].[6]

A HOMECOMING FOR HERESY

In 335 a council met in Jerusalem and admitted Eusebius of Nicomedia to communion. This decision, ostensibly an act of grace extended by the winning party to the losers, would prove disastrous for the peace, purity and unity of the fourth-century Church. Apparently, Constantine could not foresee the consequences of this generosity. From the beleaguered Emperor's perspective, the Nicene Creed had already become the law of the church so that debate need not be revisited. Apparently the only issue that Constantine had addressed was whether parties to the debate, having been properly punished, should be restored, and if that restoration would bring peace to the church. The fact that Arius' confession omitted the creed's essential phrase may never have been noticed by this man whose passions were primarily political. All he could see was that a gracious gesture toward those whom the Council had rejected would be welcomed by their friends, opening the door to a time when all would be together at the table – friend and foe alike – and the church would enjoy a season of peace.

WINNING THE WAR – LOSING THE PEACE

What happened to the church in Nicomedia and Jerusalem has occurred in ecclesiastical councils many times hence. In 1978, for example, the General Assembly of the Presbyterian Church, the denomination's highest governing body, conducted a major debate on the subject of homosexuality. At issue was a special committee recommendation – heavily supported by key national staff and elected leaders – to accept as morally legitimate the sexual practices of homosexuals. By a huge majority, commissioners at that General Assembly rejected the special committee recommendation and approved a substitute document declaring such behavior out of accord with the teachings of Scripture. The approved statement banned persons who openly engage in homosexual relations from ordained leadership in the denomination.

The majority position on this issue was definitive. Homosexual behavior is a sin, said the Assembly. Self-avowed, practicing homosexuals may not be ordained. But those who won the debate appeared discomfited by their victory. The sentiment was expressed that Christians who win a contest should bend over backwards to treat the losing side with compassion. So, without reneging on its assessment of homosexual behavior, the Assembly added statements that called for compassionate ministries to homosexual people, opposition to any abridgment of their civil rights, and condemnation of "homophobia" (a word of undefined meaning both then and now).

Seizing opportunities implicit in these three additions, denominational leaders who do not reflect the will of the General Assembly have worked steadily to undermine it. "Compassionate ministries to homosexual people" has been interpreted by activists to mean support for networks that seek to legitimize homosexual behavior. "The civil rights of homosexual people" has been interpreted to mean "ordination rights" in the church. And "homophobia" has been defined as any attitude that results in the exclusion from ordained office of persons who engage in same-sex intimacies.[7]

Although its resolve has been tested on several occasions over the succeeding years, the General Assembly has consistently reaffirmed its 1978 position that homosexual behavior is a sin and that those who openly engage in it may not be ordained. But throughout the same period, staff and elected leaders in the denomination's official agencies – claiming a mandate to act based on a few scattered clauses in the 1978 document – have produced curriculum materials, promoted conferences, and supported events that undermine the General Assembly's position.

Such defiance of the will of the General Assembly by its top leadership has engendered a revolution within the denomination's congregations, resulting in the loss of members (the Presbyterian Church (USA) has dropped from 3,382,783 in 1978 to 2,698,262 in 1994), and a drastic curtailment of congregational contributions to the denomination's mission budget. The General Assembly Council and its staff are now so estranged from most Presbyterians in the pews that demands for a decentralized leadership system are coming from every sector of the denomination.

General Assemblies since 1978 have consistently defeated proposals by homosexual activists to overturn the denomination's ordination standards by huge margins, but each majority has incorporated into its decision an olive branch for the defeated caucus. In 1993 the concession called for a three-year, denominationwide study of homosexuality that provided "safe space" for homosexuals and opportunities for establishing personal relationships with them. The number of congregations that have conducted the proposed study is minuscule, but the call for a three-year study ensured that the issue would return for another General Assembly vote after the study period had passed.

The study period also provided opportunity for defiant presbyteries (presbyteries ordain ministers) and local church sessions (sessions ordain lay leaders) to ordain additional persons who openly engage in homosexual behavior. These persons have lobbied vigorously for a General Assembly decision to reverse the standards they are now violating.

Thus concessions – made by the majority as expressions of compassion for the minority – have kept the Presbyterian Church (USA) in constant turmoil over a protracted period. Instead of making the tough decision, embedding it in the denomination's Constitution and insisting on its enforcement, General Assemblies have affirmed a principle and then shied away from its implementation. The resulting confusion, frustration and anger has robbed the denomination of its integrity, alienated the membership from its leaders, and enervated its witness to the world.

TARGETING ATHANASIUS

Back from exile, Arius and his supporters reorganized their forces and went after the man whom they blamed for their defeat at Nicaea. Encouraged by Eusebius of Nicomedia, a group of Meletians (Egyptian Church leaders) accused Athanasius of foul play on several fronts. They charged him with graft (acquiring linen tunics from the Meletians as a part of their tax obligation), destruction of sacred property (allowing – and possibly even encouraging – his assistant to smash a chalice and overturn an altar used by one of Athanasius' opponents), and being improperly elected as bishop of Alexandria (they said he was under age at the time of his election). The charges were brought to Constantine, who took them seriously, investigated them, and dismissed the case.

These matters had hardly been laid to rest when Arius' allies composed a letter to Constantine, telling him that they had new evidence that Athanasius had not only allowed but ordered the chalice smashed and the altar overturned. Then they added a far more serious allegation, one that they knew would force Constantine to reopen the case. They accused Athanasius of murdering Bishop Arsenius. Waving a bloody hand before crowds of supporters, they said that after killing Arsenius, Athanasius severed his hand in order to make use of it for magical practices.

Constantine called for these matters to be adjudicated by a council of Athanasius' peers. Immediately, the political pot began to boil. Eusebius of Nicomedia made preparations to attend and so did his allies, the Meletians in Egypt. Aware that the cards were being stacked against him, Athanasius decided to boycott the meeting. Instead, he dispatched his deacons to investigate the alleged murder of Arsenius and they found the bishop, very much alive, hidden in the city of Tyre.

SLEIGHT OF HAND

Socrates, a lawyer in Constantinople who wrote a history of the Church from 305 to 439, recounts a dramatic scene in which Athanasius confronted his accusers. He says that as soon as Athanasius appeared before the assembly, his accusers exhibited the hand, and repeated their charge. Athanasius then asked if his accusers actually knew Arsenius, and several replied that they did. Thereupon, reported Socrates,

> He caused Arsenius to be introduced, having his hands covered by his cloak. Then he again asked them, 'Is this the person who has lost a hand?' All were astonished at the unexpectedness of this procedure, except those who knew whence the hand had been cut off; for the rest thought that Arsenius was really deficient of a hand, and expected that the accused would make his defense in some other way. But turning back the cloak of Arsenius on one side, Athanasius showed one of the man's hands. Again, while some were supposing that the other hand was wanting, [Athanasius] permitted them to remain a short time in doubt. Afterward he turned back the cloak on the other side and exposed the other hand. Then addressing himself to those present, he said, 'Arsenius, as you see, is found to have two hands: let my accusers show the place whence the third was cut off!'[8]

NEW CHARGES

But the campaign against Athanasius had only begun. The Arians intensified it by instigating new charges. This time their surrogates accused him of violence against persons of lesser rank, especially the Meletians in Egypt. They argued that Athanasius had forced his subordinates into submission by threatening physical abuse. Witnesses were lined up to testify that he had beaten them.

Weary with the constant turmoil that surrounded Athanasius, Constantine called yet another council, the Council of Tyre, and ordered that all parties to the dispute, including Athanasius, attend. Athanasius was deeply distrustful of Flavius Dionysius, the man whom Constantine appointed to preside over the proceedings, and he complained bitterly over the fact that in pre-trial depositions he was not allowed to face his accusers.[9] Nevertheless, under imperial orders, he appeared at the meeting.

THE COUNCIL OF TYRE

At the Council of Tyre (335), Athanasius' enemies produced a long list of allegations. They said that he had imprisoned disobedient subordinates and had physically assaulted persons who had opposed his illegal election as Bishop of Alexandria. The Meletians even defended their disproved accusation that Athanasius murdered Arsenius by saying that while the killing admittedly did not happen, it was reasonable to assume that it could have happened in the light of Athanasius' alleged violent treatment of fellow bishops. In support of that contention, they charged that a bishop named Plusian, who had worked for Athanasius, had burned Arsenius' house after having "fastened him to a column, and maltreated him with thongs, and then imprisoned him in a cell."[10] They argued that had Arsenius not escaped from the cell through a window, he would have died in the manner that they had originally reported. Adding a charge that was certain to whet Constantine's interest, some accusers even said that Athanasius had been seen hurling stones at the Emperor's image.

STACKING THE DECK

The Council commissioned an inquiry, naming to the investigating party persons who were likely to favor the Arians. When the commission returned to Tyre, it announced its conclusion that

Athanasius had in fact ordered the chalice broken and the altar upended. As to the truth of other charges, they complained that Athanasius had so intimidated the witnesses that they were afraid to corroborate charges that had been brought against him. They recommended that Athanasius be found guilty on the one charge of destroying sacred church property.

Knowing that his chance of receiving a fair trial was nil, Athanasius, under cover of darkness, slipped out of the building, boarded a raft and floated past the soldiers who guarded the harbor. He headed straight for Constantinople, intent on informing the Emperor of procedural inequities and injustices that he had suffered.

On the following day, the Council of Tyre found Athanasius guilty on four counts: (1) That he had proved himself guilty by skipping out before the trial was over; (2) That he showed lack of respect for ecclesiastical authority in that he had refused to appear before the Council of Caesarea (subsequently called off by the Emperor when the dead Arsenius turned out to be alive); (3) That his language, and that of his defenders, in the Council of Tyre was abusive and disrespectful; and (4) That although he did not break the Meletian chalice and altar, he was responsible for the incident.[11] The Council voted to depose Athanasius, and it named a successor to his bishopric in Alexandria.[12]

In a twist of irony, the historian Socrates reported that the Council voted to add the formerly dead Bishop Arsenius to its roll just before it polled its members on the question of deposing Athanasius. Socrates wryly recounted the event:

> They moreover received into communion Arsenius,
> who was reported to have been murdered ... Thus,
> by an extraordinary course of circumstances the
> alleged victim of assassination by Athanasius was
> found alive to assist in deposing him.[13]

APPEAL TO THE EMPEROR

Constantine had been out of the city and was returning on horseback at the head of a great entourage when Athanasius ran into the middle of the street and blocked the procession. Defying threats from Constantine's soldiers, Athanasius pleaded for an audience with the Emperor. He told Constantine of improper procedures that had been employed to amass "evidence" against him, the fact that he had not been allowed to face his accusers, and the manner in which the commission of inquiry had been stacked with persons known to favor Arius.

Constantine immediately declared null and void the Council of Tyre's deposition of Athanasius and dispatched a letter to all bishops who participated in the decision:

> In your mutual love of contention, which you seem desirous of perpetuating, you disregard the consideration of those things which are acceptable to God. It will, however, I trust, be the work of Divine Providence to dissipate the mischiefs resulting from this jealous rivalry, as soon as they shall have been detected; and to make it apparent to us, whether ye who have been convened have had regard to truth, and whether your decisions on the subjects which have been submitted for your judgment have been made apart from partiality or prejudice. Wherefore it is indispensable that you should all without delay attend upon my piety, that you may yourselves give a strict account of your transactions.[14]

A response was already on its way. When Athanasius escaped their trial, the bishops assumed he would seek refuge with the Emperor. Thus, they dispatched a delegation, including Eusebius of Nicomedia and Eusebius of Caesarea, to defend their verdict.

But when the bishops arrived, they discovered that Constantine had already nullified their action. Apparently concluding that it would be futile and probably dangerous to challenge imperial authority, they took a different tack. The bishops laid before Constantine a new charge, namely, that Athanasius had threatened to impound corn ships at the docks in Alexandria. The charge, if it could have been proven, was serious, for the imperial city was dependent upon the free flow of ship traffic from Alexandria.

Athanasius denounced the accusation as frivolous, saying not only that he did not do such a thing, but that the very idea that he could have done so was preposterous. He argued that as a bishop, he would not have had the authority to impound the shipping trade. Eusebius countered with charges that Athanasius merely pretended to be a poor priest when he was, in fact, a very rich and influential man who could have stopped the grain ships if he chose to do so.

Exploding with rage, Athanasius lashed out at Constantine for taking the charge seriously. He threatened the Emperor, saying that if Constantine found him guilty of these trumped up accusations, he would surely face the judgment of Almighty God. Offended by Athanasius' outburst, Constantine banished the bishop to Gaul.

The effect of Constantine's action was legal rather than ecclesiastical. The Emperor had already declared the Council of Tyre's deposition of Athanasius null and void. Thus Athanasius remained the bishop of Alexandria, but he was now a bishop in absentia. Athanasius' authority to rule the daily affairs of his city had been, for all practical purposes, suspended.

POLITICAL CHANGE

In 337 Constantine the Great died, and his empire was divided among his three sons, Constantine II, Constantius and Constans. Constantine II ruled Gaul and parts of Africa. An ardent admirer of Athanasius, he notified the bishop that he could return home. Athanasius did so, and was greeted by a great celebration as he re-entered the city of Alexandria.

Egypt and the rest of the East were ruled by Constantius, who was inclined toward the Arian faith. Immediately on Athanasius' return to Alexandria, the Arians formed an alliance among three groups: the Arians, the Jews and the pagans, each of which had its own reasons for wanting to get rid of Athanasius. The alliance fomented discord that resulted in riots in several areas of the city. That gave Constantius a reason to intervene. He declared martial law and dispatched an officer to restore public order. Warned that he was on the verge of being arrested, Athanasius escaped, taking refuge in Rome, where he was under the jurisdiction of Constantine's third son, Constans, a strong supporter of the Nicene Creed.

While living in Rome Athanasius became a scholar in exile under the tutelage of Julius, the Bishop of Rome. Here he learned Latin and developed strong friendships with clergy leaders in the

Western part of the empire. Encouraged to do so by Julius, Constans called a council in Sardica and asked it to review all charges that had been made against Athanasius by bishops in the East. The Council did so, acquitted him of every charge, and formally lifted the sentence that had been imposed upon him by the Council of Tyre. Then Constans wrote his brother Constantius, asking him to restore Athanasius to his see in Alexandria and threatening to send his armies against him if he failed to do so.

Up to his ears in a war with the Persians, Constantius was in no mood to fight his brother, so he sent Athanasius an invitation to come home. But the bishop was wary, knowing that Constantius' invitation was anything but sincere and that it could be easily reversed. Constantius had to write three letters of assurance before Athanasius agreed to return. As the bishop entered Alexandria, Christians ran out into the road, welcoming him in a joyful demonstration. For nine years Athanasius ruled his bishopric without significant opposition.

ANATHEMA FOR ATHANASIUS

In 350, Constans was killed. Shortly thereafter, Constantine II died. Constantius, now the sole ruler of the empire, declared war on the Nicene Creed, and he personally directed a campaign to rid both church and state of its principal defender, Athanasius. Constantius ordered bishops in both the East and the West to convene ecclesiastical councils, and he encouraged them to depose all bishops who had supported the Alexandrian leader. With the exception of Alexandria, where Athanasius enjoyed enthusiastic support, Constantius' task was easy in the East, where Arianism had gained a strong foothold. In the West, however, most notably in Rome where Bishop Liberius ruled, Constantius encountered heavy resistance.

Constantius established a beachhead in the Council of Sirmium, which in 351 voted to depose Athanasius. The Council dispatched a letter throughout the West, calling for concurring signatures from bishops who had not attended the council meeting. Constantius himself sent officials to visit bishops in Italy, Gaul, Spain and Britain, compelling them to add their names under threat of exile. Faced with the choice of signing the document or forfeiting their sees, bishops throughout the West acceded to the Emperor's demand.

But Liberius, the influential bishop of Rome, was not so easily persuaded. He wrote to the Emperor, urging him to call another council meeting in which the bishops could discuss the proposed condemnation of Athanasius based on the criteria of Christian faith and not under the threat of physical coercion.

THE COUNCIL OF MILAN

Constantius called the council, which met at Milan in 355. It was clear from the start, however, that this was not to be a time of theological discussion. The meeting opened with an imperial demand that all present sign the document that condemned Athanasius. Following Liberius' lead, Bishop Eusebius of Vercellae made an impressive attempt to turn the discussion from politics to faith. According to historian Timothy Barnes, a credible account of the Council discussion was written by Hilary of Poitiers within three years of the meeting. Barnes relays that account:

> Hilary of Poitiers reported that when Eusebius of Vercellae was pressed to sign the condemnation of Athanasius, he replied that agreement ought to be reached first on the orthodoxy of the bishops present, since he had heard that some were 'polluted with heretical corruption.' He then produced a copy of the Nicene Creed and professed himself willing to fulfill the demands made of him if everyone subscribed to this creed. Dionysius of Milan took the paper and began to append his assent. Valens snatched the pen and paper from his hand, shouting that that was not on the agenda. The episode became known and provoked resentment in the city. The bishops, therefore, repaired to the imperial palace and – here, unfortunately, the fragmentary narrative breaks off. [15]

This account of proceedings at the Council of Milan could well have been written of church meetings today. Spokespeople for reform movements in all of the mainline denominations complain of their difficulty in getting church officials to discuss the subjects that really matter. In Milan, Constantius' ecclesiastical surrogates insisted that Athanasius be judged on superficial matters, e.g., his "guilt" over having conducted an Easter worship service in a building that had not yet been officially dedicated. They refused to allow the discussion to focus on the truth of Athanasius' beliefs. Almost without exception, when Athanasius' supporters attempted to turn the focus to the Nicene Creed they were ruled out of order.

Parallels in the life of the Presbyterian Church (USA) today are striking. When issues of faith are raised at many presbytery, synod and General Assembly meetings the resulting discomfort experienced by those present is obvious. Invariably, someone will raise a point of order and shift the discussion into issues of parliamentary procedure and organizational concerns. When this occurs, theological concerns are transposed into political discussions.

CONVERSION BY COERCION

Realizing that the bishop of Rome was a key figure in the ecclesiastical resistance, Constantius went after Liberius with a vengeance. The Emperor ordered the prefect of Rome to arrest Liberius and deliver him to the imperial court in Milan. There the Emperor and bishop met face to face. Barnes reports the incident:

> When Liberius persisted in his recalcitrance, he was sent to Beroea in Thrace until such time as he should agree to append his name ... to the synodical letter of the Council of Sirmium (Hist. Ar. 41.3). In his place the archdeacon Felix was consecrated bishop of Rome by the prescribed trio of bishops (Hist. Ar. 75.3).[16]

Barnes says that although the clergy of Rome had all sworn a public oath never to accept any other bishop as long as Liberius lived, they crumbled under imperial pressure and acknowledged Felix as their legitimate bishop.

In short order, most of the remaining bishops, both East and West, signed the condemnation of Athanasius. That gave Constantius the ecclesiastical imprimatur that he felt he needed to make a direct move against the bishop. In February 356, while Athanasius and his people were keeping vigil on the eve of holy communion, an army marched into Alexandria to arrest Athanasius. Unruly soldiers broke down the cathedral doors and routed worshipers. In the melee, women were raped and people were trampled by frightened crowds trying to exit the building. Athanasius escaped.

All towns and villages in the area were searched, but without success. Athanasius remained hidden for six years. Much of the time he was in Alexandria itself, where the people were loyal to him. At times when searches in the city were intense he traveled far up the Nile, where he found protection among cave-dwelling monks. This period proved to be one of the most productive times of his life. It was during these years that he produced almost half of his writings, documents recounting the history and theology of the time that have become treasures for the Christian Church.

HELP FROM A HEATHEN

Constantius died in 361 and was succeeded to the throne by Julian ("The Apostate"). Having been educated in Athens, Julian was thoroughly committed to Greek philosophy and to the revival of that culture's pagan religions. Unwilling to risk a direct attack on the Church, he devised a plan to destroy it from within by fanning the fires of the post-Nicene controversy. Julian recalled all bishops who had been deposed by his predecessors, assuming that this would generate internecine warfare between them and the bishops who had replaced them.

Twelve days later, Athanasius appeared in Alexandria. But there was no one there to dispute his return, for the Arian bishop who had been appointed to replace him had recently died at the hands of a mob. Athanasius called a council of Egyptian bishops. The summons was temperate and peacemaking in tone, and many bishops responded. Athanasius offered warm greetings to all, with a special word of forgiveness and welcome to those who had under coercion signed letters of condemnation against him. The event proved to be a great movement toward reconciliation.

This was reconciliation in the best sense, for it was brought about by a process in which politics played second fiddle to theology. The Nicene Creed was reaffirmed by all parties, and, on the basis of that shared faith commitment, relationships were restored.

THE "LITTLE CLOUD" THAT PASSED

Frustrated over the failure of his scheme to divide the Church further, Julian moved to rid the empire of Athanasius. In a letter to Athanasius, Julian said that he had never intended to restore him to his bishopric when he issued the edict that brought him home. He ordered Athanasius to leave Alexandria at once, and not to stop until he had crossed the borders of Egypt.

As Athanasius prepared to enter this, his fourth exile, he said to the people, "Let us retire for a brief while, my friends: 'Tis but a little cloud, and soon will pass."[17] The cloud may have been little but it was definitely stormy. Socrates writes that Athanasius fled from Alexandria with Julian's soldiers in hot pursuit. Reconciled to the fact that he could not outrun his foes, Athanasius conceived a trick. He sent his companions back with instructions to send Julian's forces into the desert on a wild goose chase. Meanwhile, Athanasius donned a disguise, reversed his course, and took up hiding in the city of Alexandria.[18] Shortly thereafter, Julian was killed in a campaign against Persia.

Jovian came to the throne and immediately began trying to repair some of the damage done by his predecessor. He dispatched a letter to Athanasius:

> Admiring exceedingly the achievements of your most honorable life, and of your likeness to the God of all, and of your affection toward our Savior, Christ, we accept you, most honored Bishop. And inasmuch as you have not finished from all labor, nor from the fire of your persecutors, and, regarding dangers and threats of the sword as nothing, holding the rudder of the orthodox faith which is dear to you, you are contending even now for the truth, and continue to exhibit yourself as a pattern to all people of the faith, and an example of virtue. Our imperial majesty recalls you, and desires that you should return to the office of the teaching of salvation. Return, then, to the holy churches, and tend the people of God, and send up to God with zeal your prayers for our clemency.[19]

THE FIFTH EXILE

Again Athanasius returned to his bishop's chair, now sixty-eight years old. His tenure was short lived, though, for after only eight months on the throne, Jovian died. Valentinian succeeded him and chose his brother Valens to administer the Eastern portion of his empire. In 365 Valens, an Arian, ordered Athanasius to vacate his bishopric and leave the city. Although the people resisted, soldiers overcame them, and Athanasius was again forced to flee for his life.

In only a few months, Valens realized that he had made a monumental error. Athanasius had the heart of the people, and in driving him away, Valens had undercut his own moral authority over one of the most important cities of his region. So he recalled Athanasius from his fifth and final exile.

"ATHANASIUS AGAINST THE WORLD"

Again the bishop returned to his city, this time without pomp and circumstance. Quietly he resumed his post as if he had never left it. For seven years he lived in the midst of a people who loved and honored him for having kept the faith at great personal sacrifice. He was active to the last, urging bishops and presbyters to contend for the faith against all forms of error.

Athanasius died at age seventy-five. He had been bishop of Alexandria for forty-five years, twenty of which had been spent in exile. Eulogizing this man of principle, his biographer, R.C. Reed, writes:

> He set his name to the creed which expressed his belief, and for fifty years he stood unswervingly by that confession. Every argument that ingenuity could invent was used to prove it false. Bishops met together in great numbers, condemned his views, and invoked upon him the curse of God. Emperors took sides against him, banished him time and again, and chased him from place to place, setting a reward on his head. At one time all the bishops of the church were persuaded or coerced into pronouncing sentence against him, so that the phrase originated, 'Athanasius against the world.' But with

all this pressure bearing on him, he changed his ground not one inch. His clear eye saw the truth once, and he did not permit his conscience to tamper with temptations to deny it. His loyalty to the truth made him a great power for good, a great blessing to the church of his own, and of all times.[20]

At rare and significant moments in history, individuals arise who embody the great movements of their day and become lightning rods for the opposition. In secular history, George Washington played this role as the American colonies fought to achieve their independence as a sovereign nation. Abraham Lincoln also rose to meet the challenge when the integrity of the Union was threatened. In each of these men, the principles of their nation were personified.

Athanasius was such a person in the life of the Church. Committed to biblical orthodoxy, he stood firm, suffering at the hands of those who would undermine the Church's integrity by worshiping an idol derived from their culture. In the history of the Christian Church, Athanasius stands tall as one who spent his life defending the truth. We are fiduciaries of that gift.

NOTES

1. Alasdair I.C. Heron, "Homoousios With the Father," in *The Incarnation: Ecumenical Studies in the Nicene-Constantinopolitan Creed*, Thomas Torrance, ed. (Edinburgh: Handsel Press, 1981), pp. 63, 64.

2. Edward Gibbon, *The Decline and Fall of the Roman Empire* (New York: Random House, n.d.), Vol. I, p. 698.

3. J. Stevenson, ed., *A New Eusebius: Documents Illustrating the History of the Church To AD 337* (London: Cambridge University Press, rev. ed., 1987), p. 353.

4. *Apologia Contra Arianos* II, V, 59 in Schaff, P., and H. Wace, eds., *The Nicene and Post-Nicene Fathers*. Series II, Vol. IV (New York: The Christian Literature Company, 1892), p. 132.

5. Stevenson, *A New Eusebius*, p. 358.

6. Ibid., p. 354.

7. Ironically, by this definition the 1978 General Assembly position, which remains the official policy of the denomination, is homophobic.

8. Socrates, *Scholasticus Ecclesiastical History*, I, 29 in Schaff and Wace, *Nicene Fathers*, Series II, Vol. II, p. 31.

9. *Apologia Contra Arianos*, VI, 72ff. in Schaff and Wace, *Nicene Fathers*, Series II, Vol. IV, p. 138.

10. Sozomenus, *Ecclesiastical History*, 2.25 in Schaff and Wace, *Nicene Fathers*, Series II, Vol. II, pp. 275-276.

11. Ibid.

12. Two of the Council of Tyre's charges bear the ring of familiarity to Presbyterians who have kept up with denominational disputes. The most frequently voiced charges against the leadership's chief critic, the *Presbyterian Layman*, are that its public criticisms exhibit a lack of respect for ecclesiastical authority and that the "tone" of its commentary is insensitive.

13. Socrates, *Scholasticus Ecclesiastical History*, I. 32 in Schaff and Wace, *Nicene Fathers*, Series II, Vol. II, pp. 31-32.

14. Socrates, *Scholasticus Ecclesiastical History*, I. 34 in Schaff and Wace, *Nicene Fathers*, Series II, Vol. II, pp. 32-33.

15. Timothy D. Barnes, *Athanasius and Constantius: Theology and*

Politics in the Constantinian Empire (Cambridge, Mass.: Harvard University Press, 1993), p. 117.

16. Ibid., p. 118.
17. Socrates, *Scholasticus Ecclesiastical History*, III. 14.1-6. in J. Stevenson, ed. *Creeds, Councils and Controversies, Documents Illustrating the History of the Church To AD 337-461* (London: Cambridge University Press, rev. ed., 1989), p. 60.
18. Ibid.
19. Athanasius, *Select Works and Letters* in Schaff and Wace, *Nicene Fathers,* Series II Vol. I, p. 567.
20. R.C. Reed, *Life of Athanasius* (Richmond: Presbyterian Committee of Publication, 1904), p. 38.

PART TWO

WHAT DIFFERENCE DID NICAEA MAKE?

Listen to Me, you who follow after righteousness,
You who seek the Lord: Look to the rock from which
you were hewn ...

Isaiah 51:1

What difference did this half-century battle make to the Church and the culture to which it bore witness? Could it have been argued then, as is often said today of those who disturb the peace by contending for the faith, that all of this controversy was to little avail and that, in fact, it may have even injured the Church's witness to the world? Why should Christians today pay any attention to this ancient controversy? In short, what is Nicaea's relevance to us?

In the following chapters we will examine some of Nicaea's gifts, not only to the Church but to the non-Christian world, for the world has benefited immeasurably from the Church's witness to the Gospel, even in places where the world has not accepted the Gospel itself. Nicaea's gifts include its insistence that Jesus Christ, of one substance with the Father, is the center of the Church's theology; an understanding that we experience salvation *in* rather than *from* this world; a theology that made possible the birth of modern science; a theology that offers a basis for human community; a theology that breathes new life into Christian worship and the arts; and a theology that provides a basis for Christian unity.

6

THE PERSON OF JESUS CHRIST

*I am the way, the truth, and the life. No one comes
to the Father except through Me.*

John 14:6

*Nicene theology reminds us that we do not worship
a mere idea. We worship a person. God was in
Christ, reconciling the world to himself. Theologians who represent the Gospel as a system of
thought miss the whole point.*

Nicaea's quintessential contribution to Christian theology was
its grounding in the person of Jesus Christ. Nicaea understood that
without a clear focus on this historical person, fully human and fully
divine, Christianity would become simply one of the world's many
philosophies. Jesus Christ, God's self revelation in flesh and blood,
is the center of Christian faith. It is he who restores us to communion with our creator. It is he who forgives our sins and stands as the
prototype of authentic humanity. It is he whom we worship and
serve, through whom we live and for whom we are willing to die.
Replace this person with a mere Christ *concept* or Christ *event,* a
source of salvation that is neither human nor divine, and you cut the
very heart out of the Gospel. Nicaea understood this and insisted that
the focus of Christian faith remain true to Jesus Christ, the one who
said, "He who has seen Me has seen the Father."[1]

It is interesting to note that where this Nicene faith took strong
root, the Church survived, and even flourished, despite the most vir-

ulent forms of persecution. On the other hand, the very areas that had welcomed Arianism proved most vulnerable when challenged later by other faiths. When Islam made its sweep through the Eastern world, Arius' theological progeny were unable to withstand it.

While there are many reasons for the West's successful resistance to Islam, one of those reasons is the fact that its people were so strongly grounded in the Nicene expression of the Christian faith. To followers of Nicaea, Christianity was not a mere system of ideas. It was about Jesus, the historical person in and through whom God had encountered his people. Few of us are willing to die for an idea, but we will die for a person whom we love. Those who inherited the faith that was articulated by Nicaea found their strength in a personal relationship with Jesus Christ. That bond became the bedrock of a faith that proved unassailable.

Evangelical theologian Bernard Ramm speaks to the crucial importance of this focus on the person of Jesus Christ:

> Jesus Christ is called a teacher in the New Testament ... However he was a unique teacher in that his teaching cannot be separated from his person. Some philosopher other than Plato could have argued for the immortality of the soul; and some mathematical genius besides Einstein could have proposed the theory of relativity. However Jesus' teaching is so joined to who he was that his teaching falls to the ground if he is separated from his teaching.[2]

CHRISTIAN UNIQUENESS VS. EGALITARIANISM

Nicaea's focus on Jesus Christ shows that the Christian faith has a radically different character from all other religions. There have been many attempts – both in the fourth century and in our own time – to concoct a universal religion based on an assumed common denominator that runs through all faiths. Decrying the violence that has fractured our world and the fact that competing religions often constitute a contributing factor in human polarization, leaders of the interfaith movement have sought a single corpus of belief that all religions can affirm. In common parlance, promoters of this approach say that all religions are rooted in humanity's pursuit of truth and should be equally honored as different roads to the same destination. One should celebrate this diversity and refrain from declaring one approach superior to another.

This egalitarian view surfaced quite dramatically in a meeting of Heartland Presbytery, a regional governing body of the Presbyterian Church (USA), on November 15, 1995. Rev. Stu Austin, a minister of the Christian Reformed Church, had requested membership in the presbytery. During the required theological examination Rev. Austin stated, "I believe that Jesus Christ is the Son of God and that He is the only way to salvation." That statement triggered a protest from Rev. Hal LeMert, who charged that Rev. Austin's faith was unacceptably narrow. "If that's your position, then I cannot vote for you," he said. LeMert later said in an interview with the *Presbyterian Layman* that he did not think it an essential tenet of the Christian faith that Jesus Christ is humanity's only access to God.

Apparently, some Heartland Presbytery officials shared LeMert's concerns. In an interview with the *Presbyterian Outlook*, Rev. John Langfitt, the presbytery executive, said Austin "demonstrated both in his statement of faith and in his answers a rather narrow understanding of the person and work of Christ." Apparently referring to LeMert's challenge to Austin's faith, Langfitt said: "There were some questions from the floor that were offered by persons with a broader understanding."[3]

The candidate's examination was approved by an overwhelming vote of Heartland Presbytery, but many of the elders present left the meeting deeply disturbed by Rev. LeMert's challenge. So the session of Roanoke Presbyterian Church drafted an overture to the presbytery that reaffirmed what Scripture teaches about Jesus Christ. "I am the way, the truth, and the life. No one comes to the Father except through Me," "There is no other name under heaven given among men by which we must be saved," and other passages were quoted in support of the presbytery resolution.[4]

The overture, which was quickly endorsed by other sessions, insisted that Heartland Presbytery reaffirm this scriptural truth and require any ordained leaders who could not affirm it either to seek counsel that would enable them to make this affirmation, or resign the ministry of the Presbyterian Church (USA).

In response, Heartland Presbytery leaders organized a colloquy that was designed to ask if belief in Jesus Christ as the only way to God is an essential tenet of the Christian faith. Papers by three theologians were presented to the presbytery. Then participants were divided into discussion groups.

Rev. Doug Shulse, a participant in one of the discussion groups, insisted that Christians not make exclusive claims for the Gospel. He said that he accepted Jesus Christ as his personal Lord and Savior, but that he did not believe people of other faiths must accept him in order to receive salvation. Other religions have their own concepts of God that are as valid for them as Christ is for Christians, he argued.

Shulse was challenged by Rebecca McElroy, a visitor from a nearby presbytery. She asked the group to consider an easily foreseeable circumstance: A member of the terrorist group Hamas carries a bomb into a room full of schoolchildren and sets off the explosion, killing everyone, including himself. This Islamic fundamentalist would have done so, she continued, believing that killing Jewish people at the cost of his own life constitutes an approach to God that would procure his salvation. Surely you cannot accept that as a valid approach to God, no matter how fervently its members pursue it, insisted McElroy.

Rev. Shulse took immediate offense. "We are not here to cast aspersions on the Islamic faith," he said. But McElroy's point was not so easily dismissed by others in the discussion group. Her words struck a nerve, for when forced to face the well-documented practices of other religions, honest people must admit that they do not really accept the egalitarian mantra that has become so popular among modern liberals. There are some religious practices that even the most radical egalitarian will not tolerate. But once that fact is admitted, the door has been opened to discernment. One then must make choices among competing faiths. And that leads one to ask on what basis a choice can be made.

Commenting on the presbytery's colloquy experience, Ellen Marquardt, associate executive presbyter, suggested that all positions stated during the meeting constituted acceptable expressions of Christian faith. "It was clear," she said, "that everyone present was deeply committed to Christ and his Church." Rev. Marquardt's commentary was a classic example of the egalitarian principle that it doesn't really matter what people believe as long as they can accept one another: "It is doubtful that any minds were changed as a result of the day's conversation," said Rev. Marquardt, "but perhaps hearts were changed as we began to know and to respect one another as individuals."[5]

Such views are widely held among mainline church leaders. They are the philosophical basis for Presbyterian Church (USA) General Assembly procedures that encourage dialogue rather than debate and that deem statements that exclude other points of view "insensitive." Ignoring problematic particulars, proponents of egalitarianism suggest that all religions be reduced to ideological systems that can then be compared for some common thread, possibly the promotion of an ideal like love or justice or truth. But this is precisely the sticking point for Christians, for Christians do not worship an *ideal*, we worship a *person*. We do not rally around a human system of thought, no matter how high-minded its ideals. Rather, we are drawn to an event, a God-given reality, a happening in history. It is that uniqueness that Nicaea affirmed, the uniqueness of the incarnation, that puts the Christian faith in a class all by itself.

NOTES

1. John 14:9.
2. Bernard L. Ramm, *An Evangelical Christology* (Nashville: Thomas Nelson, Inc., 1985), p. 15.
3. *The Presbyterian Outlook*, April 8, 1996, p. 3.
4. John 14:6; Acts 4:12.
5. *The Presbyterian Outlook*, April 8, 1996, p. 4.

7

NICENE THEOLOGY
AND THE BIRTH OF MODERN SCIENCE

*And the Word became flesh and dwelt among us ...
full of grace and truth.*

John 1:14

*In the incarnation God declared that he takes his
creation seriously. He who made the world has
come to redeem it. The world is not merely a veiled
reflection of some ethereal ideal that exists elsewhere. We seek neither a way out of this world, nor
any mystical enclave within it that would encourage
us to believe that matter does not matter. Christians
worship Emmanuel, God with us.*

ESCAPE VS. REALITY

At the root of most non-Christian religions stands the ancient
dualistic hypothesis that will not allow for any connection between
God and the material universe. Based on that premise, the world's
non-Christian religions offer chants, exercises, disciplines, incanta-
tions, rituals, and sacrifices all designed for one purpose: to release
the individual from bondage to a material world. Salvation is equated with escape.

Bishop Lesslie Newbigin, who spent most of his life on the mission field in India, observes that implicit in religions based on the
dualistic assumption is a strong sense of isolation. He points out that
even when practitioners of the great Eastern faiths worship in a

117

group setting, their activity is individual rather than corporate. Although the worshipers may be together in one place, each is engaged in his own ritualistic escape from this world into some transcendent realm.

Pointing to Hinduism to illustrate his thesis, Newbigin says

> It follows from the nature of this basic experience that the unity which Hinduism offers is rather the negative unity of tolerance than the positive unity of love. Hinduism is a way of salvation for the individual ... Hinduism has no doctrine of the Church ... It is necessarily a purely individual experience ... The unity that it offers is the cessation of strife, not the creation of a new community.[1]

Had Arius won the day, Christianity would have had no sense of the Church as a community of faith and easily could have joined other religions in offering the world little more than an additional avenue of escape from the world. But Nicaea declared that in Jesus Christ, God had initiated an intimate bond with humankind. The Creator had come to redeem his whole creation. Newbigin puts it this way:

> Christianity can retain faith in the reality and goodness of this visible world, can believe that it is the work of God's fingers and the object of his love and therefore a worthy object of our love, because Christ rose from the dead. Without that faith, the most obvious option open to us, and one obviously attractive to those in the West who have lost the resurrection faith, is the way of the Vedanta, the way which finds ultimate reality in the spiritual and sees the visible world as the veil of illusion which the wise man learns to strip off.[2]

TAKING THE WORLD SERIOUSLY

With the advent of incarnation faith, people who had formerly dismissed the material world as a cyclical, purposeless realm of illusion could now take it seriously, for the biblical view saw the world from an entirely different perspective. God had created the world and called it good. God had intentions for his creation, imbuing it with purpose. God declared his eternal connectedness with the world through the incarnation and resurrection of Jesus Christ. In Jesus, God demonstrated his purpose for humankind and reconciled a broken humanity to himself. In Jesus' resurrection, God announced his final victory over any force that would threaten to fracture or destroy his creation.

These theological affirmations, unique to the Christian community, set the stage for the development of modern science. If God created the world and called it good, then rather than seek escape from the world, Christians could look for the world to reveal the imprint of its Creator. The Christian world view made it possible to look within the created order for laws and principles, and, on the basis of these discoveries, to begin unlocking its secrets and developing its resources.

Lesslie Newbigin comments on the implications of Nicene Christianity for the birth of modern science:

> Most of the ancient religions have interpreted the movement of events in terms of recurrent cycles. The idea of linear movement in a single direction is incompatible with their deepest convictions ... This cyclical interpretation of the events of history is the most natural one if, with the ancient Eastern faiths, one holds that Reality is essentially timeless and changeless spirit. Reality is, in this view, the center of the spinning wheel, changeless and motionless. What was there at the beginning is there at the end. The appearance of change is illusion ...
>
> The modern, scientific world civilization ... contains as an essential ingredient the idea and the fact of purposive change, an idea fundamentally incompatible with the cyclical time scheme of the ancient Eastern religions ... this idea ... found its way into Western civilization from the Bible.[3]

THE POSSIBILITY OF CHANGE

The driving power behind modern science, says Newbigin, is the fundamental assumption that human life can and ought to be changed.

> Without this last element, the modern development and worldwide spread of scientific ideas and methods would be impossible ... It is indisputable that the universal dissemination of the methods of thought and action characteristic of modern Western science is indissolubly related to the belief that by its means human life can be made better, fuller, richer than it has been in the past, and that human history ought to be understood in terms of the effort to make it so.[4]

Newbigin says that in the West we are so familiar with this way of thinking we generally forget that "it runs counter to some of the deepest elements in the religious faith of at least half the human race."[5] He observes that in the past three decades, many countries that are dominated by Eastern religions have become attracted to the technology of the West and are seeking to import that technology while rejecting the theological presuppositions that undergird its development.

Parallel to that development in the East is the increasing secularization of the West by which it is abandoning the presuppositions that made its technology possible. In both cases, the resulting admixture constitutes an internal contradiction that is producing unhappy circumstances. The world has become dazzled with technological wizardry, but it finds no satisfaction in events and possessions that have no coherence. We pursue titillation from gadgets and fads, searching for something more bizarre than its predecessors, because life without meaning or purpose is boring. We flip from one television channel to another without satisfaction, for entertainment without inspiration is sterile.[6]

Devoid of its theological underpinnings, our technology treats the material world as an "other" to be conquered and controlled rather than as a substance of inherent worth to which we are intimately related and for which we have been given a divinely commissioned responsibility. The Eastern pursuit of Western technology minus the world view that made it possible, and the West's abandonment of its theological heritage, have produced what Jesus described as a food that will not fill, a drink that does not quench.[7]

THE PANTHEIST'S OPTION

A corollary to the escapist view, but still rooted in its dualistic assumptions, is the pantheist argument that God and the world are one. On its face, pantheism appears to value the material world, and it has become much in vogue as an ideological basis for modern ecological movements. Pantheistic liturgies at the Re-Imagining conference focused on bread, milk and honey, tactile experiences and bodily fluids. Conference participants took part in rituals in which they painted red dots on their partners' foreheads, recognizing "the divine" that lived within them. Their ersatz communion service was replete with sensual expression. "Sophia, Creator God, let your milk and honey flow … Shower us with your love," sang the congregation, followed by words from the worship leader: "We celebrate the sensual life you give us. We celebrate the sweat that pours from us during our labors. We celebrate the fingertips vibrating upon the skin of a lover. We celebrate the tongue which licks a wound or wets our lips. We celebrate our bodiliness, our physicality, the sensations of pleasure, our oneness with earth and water."[8]

But a closer look at this philosophy reveals that although it makes frequent reference to sensual sensations and the things of earth, it does not value those things in themselves. For pantheism, material things are but a shell within which the divine spirit dwells.

The Christian doctrine of creation, on the other hand, sees the world as an entity that has its own integrity, its own laws, and its own principles of being and becoming that can be observed, predicted, and harnessed. Contrary to the claims of pantheism, Christians believe that in creating the universe, God gave it an existence separate from himself. Although it is dependent on God, it also stands apart as a reality that is separate from God and loved by God.

Colin Gunton, Professor of Christian Doctrine at King's College, University of London, says

If God is ontologically too close to the world, the
world becomes simply a function of his being and so
is unable to be itself. Otherness – the ontological
distinction or infinite qualitative difference between
God and that which is not God – is important both
for the contingency of the created order and for the
freedom of the human person.[9]

Thomas Torrance, Professor Emeritus of Systematic Theology at
the University of Edinburgh, writes that in viewing the relation of
God to the universe we are not to view the relation either as a necessary one or as an arbitrary one. "God was free to create the universe,
but he was also free not to create it."[10] Torrance underscores the
teaching of Athanasius that

The universe flowed freely from and is unceasingly
grounded in the eternal love that God is. Although in
his complete self-sufficiency God has no need of the
universe, he nevertheless freely created it out of his
love and grace, so that the universe must be regarded
as having an ultimate rational ground in the benefi-
cent nature and love of God.[11]

Torrance says that the created order was intended by God "to be
a creaturely correlate of the fellowship, communion and faithfulness
which are manifested in God himself ..."[12] He continues

The whole *raison d'être* of the universe lies in the
fact that God will not be alone, that he will not be
without us, but has freely and purposely created the
universe and bound it to himself as the sphere where
he may ungrudgingly pour out his love, and where
we may enjoy communion with him.[13]

Torrance reminds us of Nicene teaching that while the universe
is dependent on God it is not simply an extrusion of divine reality.
Thus, there is in Nicene thought a tension between the dependence
and the independence of creation with respect to its Creator.

> God has made nature in such a way that it operates with a certain measure of autonomy ... That implies that whenever we seek to explore and understand nature we may do so only by examining nature as it actually is in itself ... And yet the very reality of this independence of nature is itself dependent, or contingent, upon God.[14]

Torrance observes that this concept, inherent in both Old and New Testament teachings, proved exceedingly problematic for those whose outlook was governed by the ultimate identification of God and nature. "The idea that this actual empirical universe, the world of sensible, physical existence, has an integrity and reliability of its own, was quite foreign to classical civilization,"[15] he says. In the final analysis, says Torrance, the doctrine of creation that made possible a scientific approach to the universe was dependent on the *homoousios*, "upon whether it was through Jesus Christ who is of one substance with the Father that 'all things were made', as the Nicene Creed laid down."[16]

TRINITY AND CREATION

Colin Gunton points to the doctrine of the Trinity as that biblical truth that enables us to understand the world in relation to God. Gunton says that God brought creation into being as an outgoing act of love. God's being-in-relation, the Trinity, constitutes a love that is expressed in creativity. Thus, creation is the outcome and the reflection of God's very existence as a relational being. It is the result of a loving act by one whose internal relations are love.

Gunton observes that no dominion is lorded over creation, nor is any dependence for its day-to-day functions required.

> Because God is, 'before' creation took place, already a being-in-relation, there is no need for him to create what is other than himself. He does not need to create, because he is already a *taxis*, order, of loving relations ... God is free to create a world which can be itself, that is to say, free according to its own order of being.[17]

GOD'S "RESPECTFUL" LOYALTY

Jeremy Begbie, Director of Studies and Tutor in Doctrine at Ridley Hall, University of Cambridge, pursues the implications of Scripture's testimony that the triune God maintains a continuing relationship with and a loyalty to his creation. He says, "The unsparing and unremitting love which took Jesus to the cross for humankind is none other than the love which maintains and sustains the created order."[18] But, Begbie continues, God's loyalty to his creation is a "respectful" loyalty.

> He gives his world a measure of independence and autonomy, allowing it 'room' to be itself, for his love achieves its ends by respecting the 'otherness of the other'... God's love for creation entails him honoring its integrity as something distinct from himself.[19]

Begbie says that God's refusal to violate the created order by the arbitrary imposition of his will, and his creation of that which is separate from and other than himself, should not be viewed as God's "self-limitation," but rather as an expression of his faithfulness to the integrity of what he has made. God's sovereignty and human free will are not mutually exclusive. Speaking from the perspective of aesthetics, Begbie utilizes concepts that apply with equal validity to the disciplines of modern science. He suggests that in dealing with the created world one must utilize methods of discovery, respect, development and redemption.[20]

Begbie notes that the Christian faith, as differentiated, for example, from pantheism, regards the created order as a thing in itself rather than an extension or emanation of the divine. Thus, the scientist approaches the material under examination with an expectation of *discovery*.

Secondly, Begbie says that the scientist will approach the material subject with *respect*. The proper approach to creation arises

> out of the conviction that God has endowed his world with an inherent order, and that our role is to allow the different levels of reality to define and

express their rationality through our engagement
with them. It is the antithesis of love to dominate
and manipulate, but of the essence of love to find
order in its object and act faithfully in accordance
with it.[21]

Begbie's categories of human involvement with the rest of creation also include development and redemption. That a human being
must engage in a respectful discovery of creation does not imply that
we must be passive in our relation to creation. Rather, we are called
to engage and encounter our world. "Respect is not the same as
absolute passivity," says Begbie.

There needs to be an interaction with creation, a
development, a bringing forth of new forms of order
out of what we are given at the hand of the Creator.
And there will be a *redeeming of disorder*, mirroring
God's redeeming work in Christ, a renewal of that
which has been spoiled, a reordering work in Christ,
a renewal of what is distorted.[22]

Jeremy Begbie associates with a network of British theologians
who are reintroducing the doctrine of the Trinity to the modern
world.[23] Their approach includes a return to Nicaea, where they discover that it was Nicaea's insistence on the essential relationship
between God the Father and God the Son (more fully developed with
an enhanced recognition of the third person of the Trinity at the
Council of Constantinople) that set forth conditions necessary for the
emergence of modern science. Nicaea discarded Arius' dependence
on Hellenistic dualism. It recognized an intimate connection between
God and creation, and it declared an essential oneness between Creator and Redeemer. It was this revolutionary affirmation of God's
self-revelation that shattered the dualistic hypothesis, allowed for
respectful discovery and redemptive intervention in the material
world, and led to the birth of modern science.[24]

NOTES

1. Lesslie Newbigin, *A Faith For This One World?* (New York: Harper & Row 1961), p. 40.
2. Ibid., p. 17.
3. Ibid., p. 19.
4. Ibid., p. 18.
5. Ibid.
6. Cf. Diogenes Allen's discussion of Kierkegaard on the aesthetic life in *Three Outsiders* (Cambridge, Mass.: Cowley, 1983), pp. 58-60.
7. John 6:32-35, John 4:13-14.
8. Re-Imagining conference ritual. Text attributed in conference materials to Hilda Kuester.
9. Colin E. Gunton, *The Promise of Trinitarian Theology* (Edinburgh: T&T Clark, 1991), p. 171.
10. T.F. Torrance, *The Trinitarian Faith* (Edinburgh: T&T Clark, 1993), p. 92.
11. Ibid., p. 93.
12. Ibid., p. 94.
13. Ibid.
14. Ibid., p. 100.
15. Ibid., p. 109.
16. Ibid.
17. Gunton, *Promise of Trinitarian Theology*, p. 147.
18. Jeremy S. Begbie, *Voicing Creation's Praise: Towards a Theology of the Arts* (Edinburgh: T&T Clark, 1991), p. 171.
19. Ibid.
20. A discussion of Begbie's application of the doctrine of the Trinity to the discipline of aesthetics appears later in this chapter.
21. Begbie, *Voicing Creation's Praise*, p. 179.
22. Ibid.
23. In 1983 the British Council of Churches established a study commission on trinitarian doctrine. This gathering, and the continuing conversations that it spawned, has produced some truly remarkable insights into the nature of the Trinity, causes for its neglect in the modern period, and the potential for Church

renewal that is inherent in the widespread reconsideration of this doctrine. The commission's 1989 report, titled *The Forgotten Trinity*, will be quoted later in this book.

24. Francis Schaeffer is another writer who presents a helpful discussion of the development of modern science in relation to biblical truth. *Escape From Reason* and *The God Who is There* are noteworthy in this regard.

8

NICENE THEOLOGY AND THE RESTORATION OF COMMUNITY

As the body is one and has many members, but all
the members of that one body, being many, are one
body, so also is Christ. For by one Spirit we were all
baptized into one body – whether Jews or Greeks,
whether slaves or free – and have all been made to
drink into one Spirit. For in fact the body is not one
member but many.

I Corinthians 12:12-14

Common among church leaders today is a concern for the loss
of community. Intractable violence in Northern Ireland, the continuing breakdown of ethnic relationships within the former Soviet
Union, and terrorism in Palestine remind us daily of recurrent forces
that fracture human communities. Within the United States, despite
three decades of civil rights legislation, affirmative action programs
and a host of public and private initiatives designed to overcome the
legacy of slavery, racial harmony still seems far from our grasp. In
fact, many civil rights initiatives appear to have deepened divisions
among the races by their promotion of reverse discrimination and
economic policies that have resulted in a huge, dependent under-
class. Soaring divorce and illegitimate birth rates are graphic
reminders that the family – viewed by traditional sociological theory
as the foundation of all social institutions – is in trouble. Many com-
munity-oriented volunteer organizations are in decline. American
society is separating into enclaves of insular-minded individuals

who, aided by advances in technology, sequester themselves behind computer screens with scant regard for community concerns.

Although modern liberals decry this balkanization of society and plead for restoration of community, the malady that they lament is, in large measure, the product of their own ideological proclivities. Their excessive emphases on pluralism and diversity have fragmented human fellowship. Nowhere is that impact clearer than in their campaign to demand public recognition of homosexuals as a class of persons defined solely in terms of their sexual behavior. Identifying people by their differences and codifying these differences in entitlement legislation, liberal activists have splintered the human community into antagonistic self-interest groups.

Politics has proven itself impotent to remedy this rapid social disintegration. This should not surprise Christians, who know that the roots of human relationships are embedded in human nature, and that they can neither be understood nor amended apart from worshipful recognition of the God in whose image human beings have been made. Were church leaders to rise above the temptation to address spiritual problems with secular solutions, they might discover the magnificent treasure inherent in their own theological heritage, a theology whose substance forms the basis for true human community. That gift was claimed for the Church at Nicaea.

GOD: A RELATIONAL BEING

Nicaea's declaration that Jesus Christ is of one essence with the Father opened the door to a fuller understanding not only of God, but of human community as well. In spelling out the essential connection between God the Father and God the Son, Nicaea declared that God is a *relational being*. Nicaea showed that while God is one in the sense that there is no other, God is not one in the mathematical sense that the Greeks had assumed and that Arius had affirmed. God is one in a dynamic, relational sense.

In its 1983-89 discussions on the meaning and relevance of Trinitarian faith, a study commission of the British Council of Churches addressed the important implications of seeing God in relational terms: "What is implied by the teaching that God is what he is as three persons in relation?" the commission asked. "The chief lesson is that if God is essentially relational, then all being shares in relation: there is, that is to say, a relational content built into the notion of being. To be is to exist in relation to other beings."[1]

Commission scholars then proceeded to show how radically this understanding of God departed from the view that had been held by Hellenistic philosophers.

> Christian theology took shape in a world where it was believed that the foundations for the world were provided by an impersonal substructure of being which was *logically* related to the superstructure. By contrast, in the doctrine of the Trinity, the Fathers developed a conception of being at the heart of which were not logical but *personal* relations. They were able to do this because the pressure on their thought of belief in Jesus and the Spirit led them to conceive of a God whose *being* consisted in communion. God is a community consisting in unbroken personal relationships.[2]

Colin Gunton, who served as a member of the BCC Study Commission, expresses it this way:

> God is indeed one in being: there is only one God. But this very oneness is not a mathematical oneness, as Arius and Greek theology had taught, but a oneness consisting in the inseparable relation of the Father, Son and Spirit, the three *hypostases* [persons] ... God is no more than what Father, Son and Spirit give to and receive from each other in the inseparable communion that is the outcome of their love. Communion is the *meaning* of the word: there is no being of God other than this dynamic of persons in relation.[3]

Gunton contrasted Arius' "essentially non-relational" view of God with the prevailing view at Nicaea: "By insisting, to the contrary, that God is eternally Son as well as Father, the Nicene theologians introduced a note of relationality into the being of God: God's being is defined as being in relation. Such is the impact of the doctrine of the incarnation on conceptions of what it is to be."[4]

THE DIVINE COMMUNITY

In the *Promise of Trinitarian Theology*, Colin Gunton demonstrates how this understanding of God as a relational being offers a theological foundation for the restoration of human community. He says that in Nicaea's insistence that God is a relational being composed of distinct persons, and in Constantinople's refinement of that concept to include more fully the person of the Holy Spirit, we see the God-intended paradigm of what community really means.

Gunton suggests that trinitarian theology specifies a crucial distinction between the individual and the person.[5]

> A person is different from an individual, in the sense that the latter is defined in terms of *separation from* other individuals, the person in terms of *relations with* other persons. To think of persons is to think in terms of relations: Father, Son and Spirit are the particular persons they are by virtue of their relations with each other.[6]

Gunton finds the trinitarian concepts of "otherness and relation" helpful in thinking of the elements that build human community. He says two central dimensions must be considered in interpersonal relations. One is the uniqueness and particularity of each person. "Even within the closeness of marriage, it is important not to speak of a union of a couple if this suggests some kind of merging into the other. To relate rightly to other people is to intend them in their otherness and particularity, to allow them room to be themselves."[7] On the other hand, says Gunton, otherness without relation is destructive. Human beings discover their full humanity only in relationship.

Reacting to the destructive forces of male domination and spousal abuse, radical feminism has emphasized separateness and individuality. "I am woman. Hear me roar!" sings Helen Reddy. But in feminism's attempt to solve one problem, it has created another that is no less serious, for, as Gunton rightly argues, otherness without relation is destructive. The feminist attempt to affirm "womanhood" as a self-sustaining entity is as damaging as a macho emphasis upon "manhood." Each leads to the rupture of community. We become ourselves only in relation to one another, for we are, at our very core, relational beings. Scripture's statement "the two become one flesh" does not refer to the destruction or elimination of either of the two persons, but to their fulfillment or completion in relation to one another. The feminist movement is correct in its insistence that gender domination is a blight on human community that must be obliterated. But the solution to that problem is found in biblical truth, not in secular self-affirmation movements.

Gunton believes that the trinitarian understanding of God as a being consisting of personal relations was the early Church's great gift toward building a foundation for human community.

> The logically irreducible concept of the person as one whose uniqueness and particularity derive from relations to others was developed by the Eastern Fathers in the heat of their concern for the loyalty of the Christian Church to the biblical understanding of God. It has continued, like an underground stream, to water the Western tradition, and continues to be desperately needed in our fragmented and alienated society. A person, we must learn and relearn, can be defined only in terms of his or her relations with other persons, and not in terms of a prior universal or non-personal concept like species-being, evolution or, for that matter, subsistent relation ...[8]

Underscoring Gunton's emphasis, the BCC study commission said of the early Church's gift:

> The implications of the development were revolutionary, for they entail, for example, that the world is not the product of some impersonal, mechanistic or logical process but the creation of a free and personal God. If the being of God consists in personal communion, it implies the priority of the personal over all other dimensions of being.[9]

MADE IN THE IMAGE OF GOD

But how does belief in God as a relational being affect human relations per se? How do we link the reality of a relational God to the dynamics of human interaction? Gunton answers that question by pointing to a fundamental tenet in biblical anthropology: Human beings are made in the image of God. But in what sense are we made in the image of God? he asks. Gunton says that Descartes and other rationalists got us off the track when they tried to locate the image of God in the human intellect. That solution, he says, is lacking on both philosophical and biblical grounds, and it throws us back to a human manifestation of the very dualism that Nicaea discarded. Since God is a relational being, three persons freely interacting in mutually constructive relations, observes Gunton, then we who are made in God's image must understand ourselves relationally as well: "If God is a communion of persons inseparably related ... then it is in our relatedness to others that our being human consists."[10]

Gunton follows a pattern established by Athanasius, who insisted that one cannot separate the creator and the redeemer. As human beings made in the image of God, we reflect that divine communal activity and are redeemed by it. This, says Gunton, constitutes the "vertical orientation" of our being made in the image of God.

Gunton says that the "horizontal orientation" of God's image is the outcome of the vertical: "What is the shape that the image of God takes in time?" he asks. "The human person is one who is created to find his or her being in relation, first with other like persons ... We find our reality in what we give to and receive from others in human community."[11] Gunton suggests that the uniqueness and distinctiveness of persons, freely relating to one another in a love that is empowered by the grace of the triune God, creates the context in which we become truly human.

POLITICAL IMPLICATIONS

The implications of this understanding of God for the development of human community are far-reaching, both for theology and for political science. Nicaea's understanding of a God who is essentially persons-in-relation created a new paradigm for understanding human social structures. It offered a theological impetus toward the idea of shared responsibility in the political order.

The BCC study commission has recognized the political implications of one's concept of God by citing the work of theologian
Erik Peterson, who wrote during the Nazi era. They note Peterson's
argument that monotheism can provide the basis for absolutist and
totalitarian political and social orders.

> Much depends upon what is meant by the oneness of
> God. If it is a purely mathematical oneness, there is
> a return to impersonal monism, in which personal
> values are swallowed in the impersonal. By contrast,
> the Trinity is concerned with relational oneness ...[12]

The commission cautions that relating theological positions and
political systems is difficult and dangerous. But it emphasized that
the way people envision the being of God does appear to shape their
understanding of the social order as well. "It is a political statement
for the Church simply to be the Church," says the commission.

> As the social reality that she is called to be, a com-
> munity whose centre should be love rather than
> coercion, she presents all political systems with a
> question about their authenticity. All political sys-
> tems, whether individualist or collectivist in orienta-
> tion, are in danger of ceasing to treat persons as per-
> sons ... The Church's calling is so to hold the Trini-
> ty in the centre that she will continue to be a
> reminder to society of its true nature.[13]

Referring to those occasions when the Church believes that it
must involve itself directly in political matters, the commission urges
it to make the theological basis for its involvement paramount in its
public witness:

> In times when the Church is rightly involving her-
> self in political matters, we believe that it is essen-
> tial for Christians to discuss politics in relation to
> the doctrine of the Trinity. The chief reason for this
> is that there is a danger that the Church will appear

to be, and may in fact be, no more than one more secular player or interest group among the many who seek to wield power and influence. If the doctrine of the Trinity is held in the centre, we are more likely to hold to ... the heart of the matter, the priority of persons, and that means persons in community over all other considerations. It is here that we shall be best able to contribute a distinctive voice to political debate, while at the same time calling attention to the dimensions of human polity that are both centrally important and most likely to be forgotten in the strife of competing interests.[14]

ECOLOGICAL IMPLICATIONS

Gunton describes the third dimension of what it means to be made in the image of God in terms of our relationship with the non-personal world. He reminds us that we do not stand "over and against the world," as if we were its technocratic rulers. Instead, the Bible describes the image of God as a part of creation that has been given a special function to perform.

It is a fact that we receive much of what we are from the world in which we are set and from whose dust we come. It is the context within which we become persons, and it, too, is in a kind of community with us, being promised a share in the final reconciliation of all things.[15]

It is not enough, then, that we human beings enjoy a harmonious relationship with one another. We are related for a purpose, namely, to perform a stewardship function in the world that enables it to reflect the glory of its creator. Thus, says Gunton, "The triune God has created humankind as finite persons-in-relation who are called to acknowledge his creation by becoming the persons they are and by enabling the rest of creation to make its due response of praise."[16]

ALL THINGS IN CHRIST

It was at Nicaea that the Church rejected Hellenistic dualism, declaring that there is an intimate connection between God and all that God has made. The key to this connection is Christ, the Son of God, who is of the same essence with the Father. It is through the person of Christ that God created and redeemed his creation. It is in Christ, working in our midst through the power of his Holy Spirit, that we find our true experience of community, not only with other human beings, but with all things that God has made.

Christians have every reason to work with others as peacemakers in the world and as stewards of God's creation, not on the basis of some pantheistic urge to be united with a tree, but on the basis of what Scripture teaches us about our bond with all creation through Christ. This act of community constitutes our proper worship of Jesus Christ:

> All things were created through Him and for Him. And He is before all things, and in Him all things consist ... For it pleased the Father that in Him all the fullness should dwell, and by Him to reconcile all things to Himself, by Him, whether things on earth or things in heaven, having made peace through the blood of His cross.[17]

NOTES

1. *The Forgotten Trinity: 1 The Report of the BCC Study Commission on Trinitarian Doctrine Today* (London: The British Council of Churches, 1989), p. 16.
2. Ibid.
3. Colin E. Gunton, *The Promise of Trinitarian Theology* (Edinburgh: T&T Clark, 1991), pp. 10-11.
4. Ibid., p. 8.
5. Cf. Alan J. Torrance, *Persons in Communion: An Essay On Trinitarian Description and Human Participation*, for a recent and helpful discussion of the structure of human participation in the triune life, which is conceived as the essential context for human speech about God. He examines the different approaches to the question of triune personhood that are found in the modern ecumenical debate. Included in his study are the theologies of Karl Barth, Karl Rahner, John Zizioulas, Catherine Mowry LaCugna, Eberhard Jüngel and Jürgen Moltmann. Torrance is Director of the Research Institute in Systematic Theology at the Department of Theology and Religious Studies, King's College, University of London.
6. Gunton, *Promise of Trinitarian Theology*, p. 11.
7. Ibid., p. 172.
8. Ibid., pp. 97-98.
9. *The Forgotten Trinity*, p. 16.
10. Gunton, *Promise of Trinitarian Theology*, p. 116.
11. Ibid., p. 117.
12. *The Forgotten Trinity*, p. 16.
13. Ibid., p. 37.
14. Ibid.
15. Gunton, *Promise of Trinitarian Theology*, p. 118.
16. Ibid., p. 120.
17. Colossians 1:16-17, 19.

9

NICENE THEOLOGY: RENEWING CHRISTIAN WORSHIP AND THE ARTS

Whatever things are true, whatever things are noble, whatever things are just, whatever things are pure, whatever things are lovely, whatever things are of good report, if there is any virtue and if there is anything praiseworthy – meditate on these things.

Philippians 4:8

All things bright and beautiful, all creatures great and small. All things wise and wonderful: the Lord God made them all.

Cecil Frances Alexander

Since the 1960s the mainline Protestant denominations in America have invested a great deal of energy into a movement called liturgical renewal. Proponents of this development complained that worship services in many congregations had become routine, rigid, colorless and stuffy. What was needed, they suggested, was lively innovation from the arts, popular culture, and the egalitarian strains of participatory democracy.

The liturgical renewalists have a point. It is possible in every generation for Christians to "settle in" with familiar patterns of worship, long after the elements that gave them meaning have disappeared. Many hymns, for example, employ lyrics that emerge from an agrarian society. "Bringing in the Sheaves" may need a bit of translation for Christians who have never traveled beyond the city limits. Bearers of the Gospel must be open to expressing its truth in the midst of a changing cultural milieu, and Christians must be discerning enough to recognize that no single form of worship is sacred. Any liturgical tradition, including those that we have inherited from earlier generations, can be corrupted. Jeremy Begbie is correct in pointing out that all things can voice the praise of their Creator. It is important, therefore, for the Church to explore the worship potential of various artistic disciplines.

Liturgical renewal, however, must never be exempt from theological considerations. Change for the sake of change invites meaningless novelty, the pursuit of the bizarre. That kind of "renewal" is as inappropriate to worship as the mantra "Reformed and always reforming" (omitting the crucial phrase "according to the Word of God") has been when applied by denominational leaders to theology.

HOW DO WE WORSHIP?

In churches of the Reformed tradition, particularly the Presbyterian Church (USA), the movement to embellish corporate worship has often paralleled attempts by denominational leaders to look to human experience rather than Scripture as the primary basis for appropriating Christian truth. Whereas the center of Reformed worship has traditionally been a thoughtful exposition of the Word, increasingly that center has been broadened to include elements that engender an emotional experience without a clear reference to the substance of Christian belief. A major danger in this approach is the tendency to see worship as something that we make happen, an accomplishment, a task that is orchestrated to bring about a particular effect.

Using the filter given to us in the biblical witness, questions should always be raised regarding the appropriateness of a proposed liturgical innovation. The introduction of helium-filled balloons, clapping and foot-stomping during the sacrament of the Lord's Supper in order to "celebrate" communion may accomplish its goal of participatory democratization, but it may also cheapen a sacred moment. Simple Jesus-centered love songs rightly express the warmth we feel in a personal relationship with our Savior, but their constant use may result in the loss of what Rudolph Otto identified as the very essence of worship, "the sense of the holy." Thus, while innovation should be encouraged, one must recognize that not all change is worthy to be called worship.

WHOM DO WE WORSHIP?

Christians not only need to evaluate the methodology of worship, we must also assess its content. It is appropriate to inquire who, in fact, is being worshiped. Presbyterian Church (USA) reaction to the Re-Imagining conference was strongest over various rituals that conference leaders identified as worship experiences. It was not so much that the conference program included speakers who made heretical statements that upset Presbyterians, but that members of their national staff and elected leadership worshiped a deity other than the God who reveals himself to us in Scripture.

All of us attend conferences in which speakers make statements with which we disagree, and most of us would not assume that a speaker's statement necessarily represented the beliefs of the audience. But corporate worship falls into a different category. Conference participants had a choice whether they would worship Sophia.

Joseph Small and John Burgess of the Presbyterian Church (USA) Office of Theology addressed this concern in their theological appraisal of the conference. In a paper prepared for denominational leaders that was later published by the *Presbyterian Outlook*, they said

> The language of worship must be shaped with theological and pastoral discernment. Prayers, litanies, hymns and liturgical actions are confessional acts of the whole gathered community. Liturgy does far more than ask individuals to consider new possibilities; it engages them in communal practice. The search for new language does not mean that every proposal is suitable for corporate worship, particularly when language is addressed to God in prayer and praise.[1]

Small and Burgess found particularly offensive the conference prayers that were offered to and in adoration of Sophia. They were not convinced by conference defenders' statements that Sophia is merely the Greek word for wisdom. "Many of the prayers went beyond using wisdom as one of the metaphors appropriately employed in liturgical address of God," they observed.

> Wisdom/sophia, both in frequency and formulation, became an alternative employed in distinction from the triune God ... Consistently extravagant language in Re-Imagining rituals transformed an attribute of God into a divine image different from 'the one true God who has been revealed in Jesus Christ' (*Book of Order* W-2.1001). Sophia was blessed, thanked, celebrated and praised in language appropriately reserved for expressing the grace of our Lord Jesus Christ, the love of God, and the communion of the Holy Spirit.[2]

WORSHIP AS PARTICIPATION

One of Nicaea's gifts to the Church is a doctrine of God that continually informs and renews our understanding of Christian worship. Reformed theologian James Torrance, who recently retired as Principal at the University of Aberdeen in Scotland, differentiates between an Arian approach to worship and an incarnational approach. The Arian view, says Torrance

> is that worship is something which *we* do, mainly in Church on Sunday. *We* go to Church, *we* sing our psalms to God, *we* intercede for Northern Ireland or the Middle East, *we* listen to the sermon (too often simply an exhortation), *we* offer our money, time and talents to God.[3]

Torrance says that this kind of "man centered" worship is, in practice, unitarian, because it has no doctrine of the Mediator or Sole Priesthood of Christ. "We sit in the pew watching the minister 'doing his thing', exhorting us 'to do our thing', until we go home thinking we have done our duty for another week!"[4]

Torrance identifies the incarnational approach to worship as the view that "takes seriously New Testament teaching about the Sole

Priesthood and Headship of Christ, the Once-and-for-all Self-offering of Christ, life in union with Christ through the Spirit, with a vision of the Church as the body of Christ."[5] In this kind of worship, the focus is not on our action, but rather our "participating through the Spirit in the (incarnate) Son's communion with the Father."[6] With its emphasis on what God has done and is doing, this understanding of worship is not highly concerned with various questions of how *we are to perform* in worship. Rather, it "recognizes that there is only one way to come to the Father, namely, through Christ in the communion of the Spirit, in the communion of saints, whatever outward form our worship may take."[7]

Torrance says that it is in the context of worship that we see the importance of the Nicene doctrine of the incarnation. In its insistence on the essential oneness of the Father and the Son, Nicaea proclaimed a doctrine of God-in-communion. "Our worship is seen as the gift of participating through the Spirit in Christ's communion with the Father."[8]

What this means for us is that even when we are engaged in an act of worship, we are never acting alone. Christ through the Spirit is acting in us. As Paul writes, "God has sent forth the Spirit of His Son into your hearts, crying out, 'Abba, Father.' "[9] Our words are His words speaking through us. This participatory movement is also seen in Romans:

> Likewise the Spirit helps us in our weakness; for we
> do not know how to pray as we ought, but the Spirit
> himself intercedes for us with sighs too deep for
> words. And he who searches the hearts of men
> knows what is the mind of the Spirit, because the
> Spirit intercedes for the saints according to the will
> of God.[10]

WORSHIP AND THE ARTS

Jeremy Begbie suggests that the incarnation has powerful implications for our approach to the creative arts. In *Voicing Creation's Praise*,[11] Begbie describes the devastating effects of post-Enlightenment theory on the arts and he suggests that bright aesthetic opportunities await those who take the doctrine of the Trinity seriously.

Begbie sees in the Enlightenment, which he describes as a retrograde return to ante-Nicene dualism, a reason for the blight that has infected much of what passes for art in the modern world. He describes much of modern aesthetics in terms of alienation. Rooted in a narcissistic infatuation with the self, modernism has used art as an opportunity for the antisocial expression of private feelings. Art, then, becomes nothing more than "personal taste." It has no meaning beyond itself. It has no purpose in the human community. It is immune to questions of truth. It does not take seriously the medium with which it works, but, rather, constitutes an assault on that medium by the emoting artist. The artist arrogantly manipulates his medium, imposing form on it, believing that there is no inherent order in the thing itself. Ultimately, art slides down the slope of nihilism, becoming little more than the public expression of private passions.

Begbie entertains hope for a rebirth of the arts that results from a renewed emphasis on the Gospel. Like modern scientists who have found in God the Father, Son and Holy Spirit a dynamic center for their exploration of the created order, Begbie finds in the Trinity the basis for a rejuvenation of human creativity. That doctrine, he says, overcomes any tendencies toward a dualism that would result in a discontinuity between ourselves and our environment.

Because Christians worship a God who created the universe out of a love that was made known personally in Jesus Christ, we can look to his creation with affectionate regard. The artist can appreciate the order and beauty that is inherent in what God has made, and can relate to and celebrate that perception. Recognizing that sin is inherent in all things, the artist can also express judgment toward those aspects of the created order that demonstrate dissonance. He can penetrate disorder, just as God did through the incarnation, and he can relate to it redemptively, bringing form out of chaos, good from evil, life over death. Just as the Creator relates to his creation lovingly, so the artist respects his medium and works to develop it in ways that praise its Creator. Just as God in Christ created, redeemed and sustains his creation in a continuing relationship of love, so the artist understands himself to be in relationship with God, other members of the human community and the whole of God's creation, participating with the triune God in "voicing creation's praise."

NOTES

1. Joseph D. Small and John P. Burgess, "Re-Imagining: A Theological Appraisal," *Presbyterian Outlook*, March 7, 1994, p. 11.
2. Ibid., pp. 11-12.
3. James B. Torrance, "The Vicarious Humanity of Christ," in *The Incarnation: Ecumenical Studies in the Nicene-Constantinopolitan Creed*, Thomas F. Torrance, ed. (Edinburgh: The Handsel Press, 1981), p. 127.
4. Ibid., p. 128.
5. Ibid.
6. Ibid.
7. Ibid., p. 129.
8. Ibid., p. 130.
9. Galatians 4:6.
10. Romans 8:26-27 (Revised Standard Version).
11. Jeremy Begbie, *Voicing Creation's Praise: Towards a Theology of the Arts* (Edinburgh: T&T Clark, 1991), pp. 186-198.

10

NICENE THEOLOGY AND THE UNITY WE SEEK

Now, therefore, you are no longer strangers and for-
eigners, but fellow citizens with the saints and mem-
bers of the household of God, having been built on
the foundation of the apostles and prophets, Jesus
Christ Himself being the chief cornerstone, in whom
the whole building, being fitted together, grows into
a holy temple in the Lord.

Ephesians 2:19-21

The modern Church has devoted much energy to the quest for
Christian unity. Concerns raised by Christian missionaries who
found denominational divisions largely irrelevant to their evangelical task and who experienced difficulty explaining the Church's
many institutional manifestations to new Christians led denominational leaders to launch what in time came to be known as the ecumenical movement. In its inception, this movement, particularly as it
was expressed through the early organization of the World Council
of Churches, focused on matters of faith. The intent was to discover
those essential elements of the Gospel that all Christians can affirm.
The initial idea was to demonstrate to the world, mainly through corporate public worship, that our oneness in Jesus Christ overshad-
owed any particularities we might manifest in matters of non-essential doctrine or polity.

In the 1950s, when denominational leaders, under the influence
of Enlightenment ideology, began to redefine the Gospel in political
terms,[1] the ecumenical movement underwent a radical shift. Increas-

ingly it was envisioned as a movement toward corporate mergers of ecclesiastical institutions. Denominational politicians argued that they could wield greater influence on secular governments if they spoke with a single voice. The biblical teaching of *organic* union (our membership in the body of Christ) was replaced by a desire for the *organizational* union that is reflected in ecclesiastical mergers.

In an attempt to implement this merger in the United States, two top denominational leaders, Bishop James Pike of the Episcopal Church and Eugene Carson Blake, Stated Clerk of the United Presbyterian Church, produced a plan of union in the 1950s that became known as the Blake-Pike proposal. Conversations rising out of that proposal spread among leaders of other so-called mainline denominations and led to the organization of a "Consultation on Church Union" (COCU). The consultation produced a plan of union for several of the major Protestant denominations in the United States. National staff members in the various denominations were solidly committed to COCU and participated significantly in plans for its envisioned organizational mergers. Although the plan received accolades from top officials in the participating organizations, it was soundly defeated when it was presented to the people for a vote.

Bloody but unbowed, the COCU organization has continued to exist, largely due to support from national church staff bureaucracies that are intent on seeing their agenda resurface. In the meantime, heavy financial support has been channeled by denominational leaders into the World Council of Churches and the National Council of Churches, the two organizations that national church leaders have identified selectively as the world's most visible expression of Christian unity.[2]

Recognizing the political realities that were so clearly demonstrated in the rejection of their plan of union, COCU leaders wrote a new draft in 1988 that altered some of the earlier language. Declaring that its revised plan is not a merger but a "reconciliation of ministries," COCU has come back before its sponsoring denominations for another vote. Critics argue that the change is semantic and that COCU's latest plan is merely a veiled, last-gasp merger attempt by failing denominational bureaucracies. Although it may be provisionally adopted by some of the national governing bodies where staff members effectively control the political process, the chance that

COCU's plan will be embraced by the people of is member denominations is regarded by most observers as exceedingly small.

By many objective measures, COCU and the World and National Councils represent colossal failures in the ecumenical realm. Is there an alternative hope for the visible unity that Christians seek? Certainly. When denominational leaders eschew politics and seek an authentic basis for Christian unity. They can find no better place to begin than in our common Christian heritage, for it is not by accident that the Nicene Creed emerged from the first "Ecumenical Council."

BAPTISM INTO THE BODY OF CHRIST

In contrast with attempts by Enlightenment-oriented denominational leaders to achieve Church unity *via* ecclesiastical politics, Thomas Torrance tells us that the key to understanding the Church, and therefore the locus of its unity, lies in Nicaea's *homoousios*. That doctrine of Christ, says Torrance, must govern the doctrine of the Church, which is the Body of Christ, the incarnate Son.

> Since Sonship of Christ falls *within* and not outside the Godhead, everything we say of the Church must be consistent with the consubstantial oneness between the Son and the Father and be an expression of the union and communion between God and man effected in the incarnate life and reconciling work of the Mediator. That is to say, the doctrine of the Church must be expounded in terms of its *internal relation*, and not some external relation, to Jesus Christ, for it is in Christ and his inherent relation to the Father and the Holy Spirit that the essential nature of the Church is to be found.[3]

Essential to the early Church's understanding of itself, says Torrance, is the sacrament of baptism, that act in the name of the Father, Son, and Holy Spirit that is a sign and seal of our cleansing, of our engrafting into Christ, and of our welcome in the household of God. Christ's baptism, signed and sealed by our own baptism in his name, is the link by which we are drawn into the very being of God, the divine communion we call the Trinity, which lies at the very heart of the Church. This is not to suggest that the physical act of baptism is the means of our salvation. Rather, the act is the sign and seal of that which God in Christ has done.

Torrance says that when Jesus Christ submitted to baptism at the river Jordan the essential linkage was made manifest:

> At the Jordan it was our humanity which was baptized in him, so it was our humanity that was crucified and resurrected in him. When he died for us and was buried, we died and were buried with him, and when he rose again from the grave, we were raised up with him. That is the truth sealed upon us in 'one baptism' ... The central truth of baptism, therefore, is lodged in Jesus Christ himself and all that he has done for us within the humanity he took from us and made his own, sharing to the full what we are that we may share to the full what he is. Baptism is the sacrament of that reconciling and atoning exchange in the incarnate Saviour. When we understand baptism in that objective depth, we are directed away from ourselves to what took place in Christ in God.[4]

ARIAN VS. NICENE VIEWS OF THE CHURCH

Torrance points out that this intrinsic connection between "one baptism and one faith" was so firmly embedded in the thinking of Nicene theologians that they refused to accept Arian "baptism" ceremonies as Christian, "for it was not baptism in the name of the Triune God, but in the name of the Father and two creatures, or in the semi-Arian case, in the name of the Father and the Son and a creaturely Spirit."[5]

Whether one adopts the Arian or the Nicene view of the relationship between the Son and the Father has major implications for one's view of the Church. Torrance reminds us that Arianism held that the relation between the Son and the Father "was merely of an external or moral kind, contingent upon the divine will, and not internal to the being of the Godhead."[6] As we have seen, that failure to make the essential connection between the Father and the Son left the Son entirely impotent to secure our salvation. At best, the Arian Christ is a moral leader for an organization that is nothing more than "a community formed through the voluntary association of like-minded people."[7]

Nicene theology's understanding of the relation between the Son and the Father produced a very different concept of the Church:

> Nicene theology ... held that the relation between the incarnate Son and the Father was internal to the one eternal being of God, and was not an external creaturely or moral relation but one intrinsic to the essential nature of God ...[8]

This kind of understanding, Torrance says, prevents us from viewing the Church as the mere product of human activity, as do modern liberals who often define the Church in political terms. It represents our having been brought into communion with the very being of God, an act that no mere human being can accomplish.

Nicene theology also helps us understand that the basis of the Church's unity lies in the unity of the Godhead.

> The Church throughout all its manifestations in space and time is intrinsically and essentially *one*, for it is constituted as Church through the presence of one Lord and his one Spirit ...[9]

Given this understanding of the Church, much of what passes for ecumenism today seems quite superficial. The Church will not be *made* one by virtue of human restructures and rearrangements. At the very core of its existence the Church *is* one, no matter how diverse its cultural manifestations.

To the degree that current ecumenical efforts draw us together in worshiping the triune God in whom we live and move and have our being, then there is much to be celebrated in these initiatives. But it is also clear that the mere existence of differently organized Christian groups that cluster around preferred forms of organization, different emphases on non-essential doctrine, and various cultural factors that do not bear on the meaning of the Gospel per se does not constitute an offense for which a remedy is required. On the contrary, one could argue that in light of the fact that all human institutions are sinful, the Church may be made healthier by the checks and balances implicit in its various cultural manifestations. Certainly, the phenomenon of multiple denominations that commune with one another around the Gospel, stands as a positive witness to the freedom and diversity that can occur within the one body of Christ.

TRINITARIAN ECUMENISM

That point has been underscored by the British Council of Churches' Study Commission – itself an ecumenical organization. The group asks if the modern Church understands itself "sufficiently in the light of the Trinity, and whether questions about its institutional origins and legal unity have not rather predominated."[10] The commission concludes that an emphasis on the doctrine of the Trinity would help heal divisions within the Church that are caused by an emphasis on one person of the Trinity to the exclusion of others. Suggesting that appeals to "Father-only" images are often associated with power lust and domination; appeals to "Jesus-only" images lead to moralistic activism or individualistic pietism; and "Spirit-only" images lead to introspective escapism or charismatic excess, the commission encourages council members to institute "trinitarian controls" on their ecclesiology.

Concerned that the Church should be a community before it is an institution, the British commission suggests that the importance of the Trinity for the Church's self-understanding is twofold:

> By stressing the fact that God's being consists in community, it asserts the theological priority of community over institution or anything impersonal. (The Church has always behaved worse when she has likened herself to an empire or understood herself as primarily a legal institution.) The Church must cease to be looked on primarily as an institution and be treated as a *way of being*. The Church is primarily *communion*, i.e., a set of relationships making up a mode of being, exactly as is the case of the trinitarian God.[11]

Second, by stressing the action of the Spirit as of equal importance to that of the Son, it makes it possible to emphasize God's present as well as his past action in constituting the Church and along with this the eschatological, future oriented, dimensions of ecclesiology. The Church will thus cease to be regarded as a historically given reality – an institution – that is a provocation to freedom. She will be regarded at the same time as something constantly constituted, i.e., emerging out of the co-incidence and con-vergence of relationships freely established by the Spirit.[12]

NICENE THEOLOGY AND INTERFAITH RELATIONS

It will appear strange to some that mention of interfaith relations would be included in a chapter on Christian unity. From the perspective of semantic consistency, such concerns would be well-founded. The inclusion, however, is purposeful, for it is intended to call attention to increasingly frequent but misguided attempts by current church leaders to employ "ecumenism" and "interfaith relations" interchangeably. Earlier in this book we mentioned the fact that under intense criticism for their sponsorship of the Re-Imagining conference and its decidedly non-Christian rituals, Presbyterian leaders justified their participation by calling it an "ecumenical event." Similarly, when challenged for having co-sponsored a conference for college students whose "Bible study" leader was Rita Nakashima Brock (Brock, also a platform speaker at the Re-Imagining conference, declared in that event that she does not believe in a transcendent God), Rev. James Brown defended the decision by declaring that the conference was "ecumenical." Brown said that it would have been "inappropriate" for Presbyterian participants on the planning team to have vetoed a decision made by the whole group.[13]

Similar attempts to blend Christian and non-Christian affirmations in the name of unity have been made by leaders of the World Council of Churches. (Technically, the organization's full title includes "Jesus Christ.") The Council's "Ecumenical Assembly" in Canberra, Australia, included among its rituals a ceremony in which participants passed through smoke as they entered the worship tent.

The smoke ceremony is a pagan cleansing ritual intended by "indigenous people" to drive away evil spirits. Inside the tent, delegates watched as World Council worship leader Chung Hyun Kyung immolated a page of words in an attempt to transport a vaporous message to her dead ancestors.

The fact that such pagan rituals occur hardly constitutes a surprise for anyone. But the fact that they have been included in "ecumenical Christian worship" raises significant questions. Those who have observed the patterns of World Council of Churches leadership in recent years understand that these inclusions are not accidental. They represent the commitment of this organization's top leadership to a more "inclusive" self-understanding, one that blurs any distinction between Christian and non-Christian theologies.

At a January 31, 1995, meeting of the Latin American Council of Churches in Concepción, Chile, Nancy Cardoso, a Brazilian theologian, called on the churches to "leave behind the idea of fundamental principles" in order to reach a mutual understanding with peoples of other religions on the continent." Cardoso told the delegates that the Church must learn to "coexist with a plurality of religious experiences," and it must become accustomed to the Latin American reality of many gods and goddesses." She criticized "arrogant and manipulative Christologies and ecclesiologies belonging to the religiosity of the so-called Christian people."

"We must re-invent the discourse, even on God, so that our ears and sensibilities are not offended every time we refer to the divinities to whom worship is offered throughout the continent," she said. Cardoso asked if the time had come for the Council to broaden its base by opening its membership to non-Christian religions. Using entitlement language, she bemoaned the exclusion of non-Christians as a denial of their "rights."

Attending the meeting was Konrad Raiser, general secretary of the World Council of Churches, who described Cardoso's speech as "an indication of the new framework of theological questioning that has emerged" in Latin America.[14] Raiser has suggested that the World Council may wish to consider welcoming non-Christian but humanitarian organizations into its membership as a solution to the problem of dwindling revenues.

CHRISTIAN HONESTY

As inheritors of the Nicene tradition, the first gift we can bring to interfaith relations is honesty. Any thoughtful non-Christian knows that there are distinctive marks to the Christian tradition. Christians in pursuit of human community who would deny or minimize that distinctiveness are simply not being honest, and they will gain no respect from people of integrity who represent other faiths. To the extent that Christians have sought to coerce others into the faith, we can express our disdain for the practice and our determination to avoid any such approach to non-Christians. But we are not required to act as if there is no difference between Yahweh and Baal.

Nicene theology can also be helpful in distinguishing those approaches to interfaith unity that are not appropriate to Christian faith. For example, Nicaea's representation of the Christian God as a relational being, a communion of persons, would proscribe attempts to find interfaith unity in the worship of some underlying divine substance. Christians do not worship a principle, we worship a God in three persons.

In 1993, representatives of several mainline denominations joined an interfaith gathering in Chicago called the Parliament of World Religions. Prominent among its endorsers, Rev. David Ramage, former president of McCormick Seminary, a Presbyterian Church (USA) institution, called the event, "a documentation of a new era." Pointing to the diversity of Chicago's religious landscape he said, "We live in the midst of genuine religious and multicultural reality. There is a mammoth transformation going on in religious and cultural life. Yet most people in the suburbs have blinders on."[15]

The parliament was indeed to be a demonstration of unity amidst diversity. Journalist John Coyne described the participants:

> Hindus, Sikhs, Muslims, Jains, Bahais, Zoroastrians, neo-Pagans, Indians of both the Calcutta and Rosebud variety, witches, warlocks, goddesses, and at least one old Beat poet – garbed in a great variety of robes, dresses, gowns, cylindrical Egyptian headdresses, turbans, cowls, hoods, Chicago Cubs baseball caps, at least one tam o'shanter, and in the case of Andras Arthen, a member of the Covenant of the

Goddess, a wolf's-head headdress, which he would wear to great effect on September 1, capering in the light of the full moon with his fellow wicans and wicanettes in the wold, a/k/a Grant Park.[16]

Parliament organizers hoped to agree on a concept of God that all participants could support. "I would recommend that we look beyond labels and look to principles, for labels are divisive," said Nation of Islam representative Louis Farrakhan in a platform presentation.[17] But members of the gathering had difficulty even with the word God. Father Hans Küng, who had been assigned the task of proposing a "minimalist" global ethic for the Parliament, said that affirming a belief in God would have "excluded all Buddhists and many other faith groups with different views of God and the divine."[18] So they settled on "Ultimate Reality" as a concept that proved sufficiently vague for all participants – from Presbyterian Church (USA) officials to the neo-pagans and the Covenant of the Goddess – to affirm. According to Coyne, the high point in conference discussions of the "Ultimate Reality" came when Lady Olivia Robertson of the neo-Pagan Fellowship of Isis "took a rattle and chanted in a loud voice: 'Holy Goddess Isis, Mother of all beings, come to thy children.' "[19]

This unity in pluralism event received high praise from Thelma Adair, a former moderator of the Presbyterian Church, who said, "This [event] reflects the reality of our daily life. And our churches are insulated from the reality."[20] It was also lauded for its inclusiveness by Rev. John Buchanan, minister of Chicago's Fourth Presbyterian Church and denominational leader. Buchanan has encouraged Presbyterians not to become locked into "confining statements," like "I am the way, the truth and the life; no one comes to the Father but by me."[21]

The Parliament of World Religions' idea that God is a divine substratum lying hidden behind all historical manifestations does not comport with Christian faith. The adoption of such an idea would carry us right back to the dualism of the ancient Hellenistic world, for such a God would be completely beyond our experience and wholly unknowable. As we saw in Chapter Six when discussing Lesslie Newbigin's assessment of Eastern faiths, worship of this sort constitutes a highly individualistic attempt to escape from this world. It is ironic that such a proposal would be offered as a method of achieving a sense of community on earth.

Nicene theology's emphasis on the being of God as persons in relation implies that Christians will relate to one another personally. This principle would also apply to non-Christians, for they, too, are human beings made in God's image. This would imply that we will approach others with regard for their personhood, respecting their freedom, and seeking friendships that affirm their uniqueness in relation. Because community is a strong concept for Christians who take the Nicene tradition seriously, we can participate in joint efforts with persons of other faiths to strengthen, protect, enrich and ennoble our life together. These activities offer us opportunities for conversation with our non-Christian partners, within which we can testify to the one in whose name we have entered the partnership, for we must always be prepared to give an account of our faith. Honoring the fact that he who entered the world came not "to condemn the world, but that the world through him might be saved,"[22] we understand that we now, having been made one with Christ, have been called to manifest his presence as well.

NOTES

1. The philosophical and theological manifestations of this development are discussed in Chapter 7.
2. This designation has been most unfortunate, for it has ignored the truly remarkable worldwide movements toward Christian unity that have been engendered by evangelical Christians. The Lausanne Movement, for example, has stood historically as a major ecumenical consensus among evangelicals. In Latin America, where established churches have invested their primary efforts into politics, an evangelical fervor that crosses all denominational lines has swept through many countries. In both size and significance, evangelical ecumenism has dwarfed the declining World and National Councils, yet mainline denominational leaders still refuse to recognize it.
3. Thomas F. Torrance, *The Trinitarian Faith* (Edinburgh: T&T Clark, 1993), p. 264.
4. Ibid., p. 294.
5. Ibid., p. 295.
6. Ibid., p. 277.
7. Ibid.
8. Ibid., p. 278.
9. Ibid., p. 279.
10. *The Forgotten Trinity: 1 The Report of the BCC Study Commission on Trinitarian Doctrine Today* (London: The British Council of Churches, 1989), p. 28.
11. Ibid., p. 29.
12. Ibid.
13. Brown made these comments at a meeting of the Presbyterian Church (USA) General Assembly Special Committee on Reconciliation with the Presbyterian Lay Committee on November 31, 1994.
14. Ecumenical News International, February 1995.
15. Presbyterian News Service, September 1993.
16. John R. Coyne, Jr., "Ultimate Reality in Chicago" in The *Presbyterian Layman* (Nov./Dec. 1993), p. 11.
17. Presbyterian News Service, September 1993.

18. Ibid.
19. Coyne, "Ultimate Reality in Chicago," p. 11.
20. Presbyterian News Service, September 1993.
21. John 14:6.
22. John 3:17.

PART THREE

ARIUS RETURNS

Why then has this people slidden back, Jerusalem,
in a perpetual backsliding? They hold fast to deceit
... Behold, they have rejected the word of the Lord;
So what wisdom do they have?

Jeremiah 8:5, 9

At Nicaea, fourth-century Christians bridged a great divide. Rejecting a theology grounded in the dualism of its culture, the bishops who gathered at Constantine's call aligned themselves with the Gospel that makes all things new. Insisting that God was truly in Christ, reconciling the world to himself, the Nicene theologians opened the world's eyes to a new way of knowing God and understanding itself. Their commitment to worship the Son who is of the same essence as the Father initiated unintended consequences that proved revolutionary in science, politics, ethics and the arts. *Homoousios*, that line of demarcation that had been drawn between dissident factions of a fractured communion, became the stimulus for unprecedented Christian unity and growth.

One need not probe very deeply into the life of the modern Church, however, to discover that a seismic shift has occurred, for its policies and proclamations reveal major discontinuities with Nicene faith. Although the ancient creed remains enshrined in ecclesiastical archives and is acknowledged officially by Protestant, Catholic and Orthodox communions, it is clear that in practice a major departure from Nicaea has occurred. Many church leaders refuse to affirm the *homoousios*. Many more simply ignore it, preferring the more "relevant" realities of secular and ecclesiastical politics.

How is it possible that the Nicene faith, once so vigorously declared, could have fallen into such neglect, and even outright opposition? What has happened to the world view envisioned by Nicaea, and what have been the results?

11

Arius Returns to Philosophy and Science

Who is this who darkens counsel by words without knowledge ... Where were you when I laid the foundations of the earth? Tell Me, if you have understanding. Who determined its measurements? Surely, you know!

Job 38:2, 4-5

Of the contemporary theologians who trace the rise of modern skepticism and measure its influence on contemporary theology, few have done so with the depth and clarity of Lesslie Newbigin. His insights have encouraged Great Britain's brightest minds to reconsider the truths of Nicaea and to regard Trinitarian faith with renewed esteem. In the brief overview that follows, we will pursue a path that Newbigin has charted in several of his lectures and writings, two of the most recent being *Truth to Tell: The Gospel as Public Truth* and *Proper Confidence: Faith, Doubt and Certainty in Christian Discipleship.*

The Enlightenment – a giant leap backward

In 1628, the philosopher René Descartes (1596-1650) accepted an assignment from Cardinal Pierre de Berulle. Troubled by intellectual challenges to Christian truth, the cardinal asked Descartes to develop a philosophy that would engender certainty among believers. Descartes was commissioned to prove the existence of God using a method that intellectuals would deem respectable. Ironically, the philosopher's assignment led him into a pursuit that was destined to undermine centuries of Christian witness.

Descartes initiated his quest with the determination to subject every idea, every assumed truth, to severe skepticism. Casting aside all propositions that anyone under any circumstances might doubt, he would reduce the body of knowledge to an essence that no human being could possibly question. Then he would build a system of knowledge, step by step, on the foundation of that one irreducible fact. Each layer would have to be clearly deduced from the former. In this manner, Descartes proposed to construct a system of universally valid knowledge, a corpus of truth that could be affirmed by persons of every culture.

Descartes' primary premise was that the only thing that can be known without a doubt is one's own existence as a thinker. "I think, therefore I am" was his famous dictum. Even when one doubts one's own existence, he argued, his existence is confirmed, for there must be someone who is doing the doubting. On this foundation, Descartes began to build a philosophical system, looking for additional facts that could be indubitably known. He decided that mathematics was the only purely scientific tool, for one could not doubt a geometrical equation. Whatever truth mathematics could sustain he would call knowledge. Everything else would be relegated to the category of faith.

RETURNING TO DUALISM

Descartes' methodology catapulted the Church thirteen centuries backward, for the essence of his philosophy was to re-introduce Hellenistic dualism. This is not to say that his was the first and only foray into Arian territory, for as theologians Michael Buckley[1] and Colin Gunton[2] argue, a strain of dualistic thought can be traced from the very beginning of Church history. But in Descartes and in those who would build their philosophies on his assumptions the annulment of Nicaea was fully and publicly proclaimed.

Newbigin suggests three consequences of Descartes' method. First,

> It strongly reinforced the dualism of mind and matter which had been such a debilitating feature of the classical world-view. By isolating the thinking mind as though it existed apart from its embodiment in a

> whole person and thus apart from the whole human and cosmic history to which that person belongs, Descartes opened a huge gap between the world of thought and the world of material things and historical happenings ... The mental (or spiritual) and the material are two separate worlds.[3]

The second consequence was "the divorce between the objective and the subjective poles in human knowing and the consequent polarization between objectivity and subjectivity."[4] Newbigin says that this led to the popular belief that science is the realm of objective facts and that all other claims to knowledge, e.g., art, literature, poetry, and religion, are merely subjective. He reminds us that this idea has been debunked by the best scientists of all times, but that it had a major impact on many nineteenth-century thinkers who popularized the concept and propagated "the myth that science had replaced religion as the centerpiece of modern civilization."[5]

Newbigin says that the third consequence of Cartesian thought was a dichotomy between theory and practice. Just as the mind had been separated from the body, now thought and action had no meaningful relationship. The implications of that dichotomy for ethics were extremely damaging.

The Cartesian methodology set in motion a thoroughgoing skepticism. It stimulated the development of modern science by encouraging the notion that propositional validity is determined by empirical tests. But, Newbigin insists, its greatest and most devastating impact was the fact that it created a prejudice in favor of doubt over faith.

IMMANUEL KANT – FROM FACT TO FEELING

Immanuel Kant (1724-1804) accelerated the momentum of Descartes' skepticism. Like Descartes, he was a man of faith who sought certainty for Christian truth in a time of growing disbelief. Like Descartes, the consequence of his philosophy for Christian theology, albeit unintended, was extremely damaging.

In his *Critique of Pure Reason*, Kant developed a theory of knowledge that has become known in popular parlance as his "Copernican revolution." Just as Copernicus reversed the perspective from which humans regard the solar system, so Kant inverted the epistemology of his time. Reversing the traditional process of approaching an object in nature as if that object presents itself to us, he taught that knowledge flows not from the world to the mind, but to the world from the mind. Reason places our sensations in categories of space and time. Reason assigns them meaning. One would be hard pressed to know a thing in itself, for we create what we know in the interaction of sensation and pure reason.

Kant insisted on the absolute separation of two realms that he called "the noumenal," the realm of ideas and ideals, and "the phenomenal," the realm of sensory experience that is perceived and interpreted by pure reason. He argued that while pure reason is necessary to our knowing anything in the phenomenal realm, its role is limited to this realm alone. Beyond the interpretation of sensations, reason is powerless to act.

Kant demonstrated the limits of pure reason in a series of antinomies, arguments employed to prove, and then to disprove, selected transcendental ideas. In his fourth antinomy, Kant employed reason to prove the existence of God. Then, using the same faculties of rationality, he proceeded to disprove God's existence. His conclusion was that pure reason is ill-equipped to handle matters of faith. It cannot say anything meaningful about God.

Thus Kant declared that all God language is faith language. As such, it is immune from either attack or confirmation by reason. It is through ethics and aesthetics, essentially matters of sentiment, that we find an avenue for speaking about God.

Newbigin argues that Kant's ideas have been oversimplified in public discussion. He says that as a person of faith, Kant had sought to find a place for belief in God at a time of growing skepticism, and he thought he found it in the realm of the moral law. But the problem was that once Kant had committed himself to the dualistic hypothesis, then anything one might say about God – or about the idea of the moral law itself, for that matter – was entirely subjective and, hence, divorced from truth in any objective sense. Whatever Kant's intentions, his work proved devastating to theology. The substance of Christian belief had been transferred from the realm of fact to the realm of feeling. One need not venture far into so-called Christian literature today to discover how firmly that idea has taken root.

FRIEDRICH NIETZSCHE – FROM FAITH TO POLITICS

Pursuing the Cartesian search for certainty, Friedrich Nietzsche (1844-1900) found in the essence of humanity one indubitable reality, the will to power. Nietzsche reasoned that the will to power is not only a human trait, but is the fundamental building block of the universe. He believed that it is impossible to possess any knowledge of absolutes. Nothing can be called absolutely true or false, good or evil. Only one reality exists, and that reality is raw power.

Nietzsche replaces issues of faith and morality, meaningless and idle pursuits in his judgment, with politics. Truth, if one insists on using the word, means nothing more than one's perspective: I claim my truth and you can claim yours. Morality is nothing more than preference. It matters not whether my choice is true or right, but whether I have sufficient power over others to assert it.

NEWTONIAN PHYSICS – THE MIGHTY MACHINE

Isaac Newton (1642-1727) applied the Cartesian methodology to science. With absolutes out of the way, and with no imperative to relate the material world to any realm beyond itself, Newtonian physics declared with confidence that what one sees is what one gets. The laws that govern matter are to be found in matter itself. Once those laws are discovered, one can predict the future with certainty. From the Newtonian perspective, the universe is a giant machine that operates according to fixed principles, knowable because of God's orderly creation. Through empirical studies, the scientist can unlock nature's secrets, apprehend its laws, and manipulate them in ways that will force nature to obey. Whereas Nietzsche's power manifested itself in politics, science pursued power over nature. The scientist was king, ruler of all nature.

Diogenes Allen writes of the impact that Isaac Newton's physics made on the modern mind:

> Newton's *Principia* was the crown of the new science of mechanics. Although it provoked controversy for a generation, it became for the avant-garde the beginning of a new age for humanity. Its general impact was compared to the breaking in of light, lifting the darkness, so that people could see the uni-

verse for the first time the way it really is. They saw
it as a precise, harmonious, rational mechanism,
with laws of motion which applied universally to all
matter, from the tiniest of particles to the vast heavenly bodies.[6]

Newtonian physics produced spectacular results. Modern science
developed a technology that vectored nature's forces through the tur-
bines of an enormous industrial machine. Unconcerned with questions of meaning or morality (since such matters are not properly
"scientific"), science operated on the assumption that if there is any
"ought" in the universe, it is the principle that one *ought* to do what
one is *able* to do. In a scientific application of the Machiavellian
maxim, technology declared that one's capacity to do something is
the only relevant consideration.

Newbigin reflects on the almost euphoric sense of liberation that
Newtonian science, in sharp contrast to Newton's own intentions,
unleashed:

Here was a model of reality that did not depend on
divine revelation or on faith. It was a model that any
cultivated intelligence could understand. Here was
the possibility of liberation from the ancient tyran-
nies of religion and superstition. The heavy weight
of ecclesiastical authority, backed by the threat of
supernatural sanctions, need no longer terrify.[7]

FROM PHILOSOPHY TO FAITH

What Nicaea had joined together, philosophers of the Enlightenment quickly put asunder.[8] Returning to the dualism of ancient times,
they leaped over Nicaea as if it had never happened. The ancient
polarities of being and becoming, the one and the many, reality and
illusion, soul and body, mind and matter, spiritual and corporeal were
revisited with a vengeance. Like Plato's cave-dwelling prisoners,
modern thinkers stared at shadows on the wall, impotent to commune with the reality that engendered them, if, in fact, such a reality
exists. What mattered was matter, the rationalization of human experience, and politics.

Human beings were taught that they could say nothing with confidence about any world beyond themselves. They could know only their own experiences, with no confidence that there was any substance behind the sensations that stirred their psyches. "God" – for those who felt the need to posit such a reality – was assigned to the gaps in human knowledge. Wherever human reason could not explain a phenomenon, God was named to fill the void. Thus reality was described in terms of those things that humans can know, and God got the leftovers.

NOTES

1. Michael Buckley, *At the Origins of Modern Atheism* (New Haven: Yale University Press, 1987).
2. Colin E. Gunton, *The Promise of Trinitarian Theology* (Edinburgh: T&T Clark, 1991).
3. Lesslie Newbigin *Proper Confidence: Faith, Doubt, & Certainty in Christian Discipleship* (Grand Rapids: Eerdmans, 1995), p. 22.
4. Ibid.
5. Ibid.
6. Diogenes Allen, *Philosophy for Understanding Theology* (Atlanta: John Knox Press, 1985), p. 186.
7. Newbigin, *Proper Confidence*, p. 30.
8. With Newbigin, we have suggested Descartes, Kant, Newton and Nietzsche as key thinkers along the philosophical path of post-Enlightenment rationalism. Obviously, others could have been mentioned. Readers who wish to probe this development in greater detail with find Francis Schaeffer's *The God Who Is There* most helpful, especially in his treatment of Hegel, Kierkegaard, and the existentialists Jaspers, Sartre and Heidegger. Schaeffer traces the movement of their philosophies through art, music, general culture and theology, and demonstrates that their presuppositions are the point at which they are vulnerable to the arguments of Christian apologetics.

12

ARIUS RETURNS TO THE CHURCH

*An interloper who steals property must be caught
and fairly charged as an expression of justice. Secularization is such an interloper. We have witnessed
the theft of Church property by forces alien and
inimical to the Church. Stolen property must be
reclaimed. Thieves must be brought to justice.*

Thomas C. Oden

Just as Arius sought to incorporate that philosophy into fourth-
century theology, so a host of post-Enlightenment theologians
attempt a similar accommodation today. The key has been their
grounding of Christian belief and morals in human experience. How
do I know that God is present? I feel it. How do I know that I am
following God's will? What I do feels right to me. This has meant,
of course, that like their Arian ancestors, post-Enlightenment theologians have had to make some adjustments to Scripture. Its "mythology" – defined as that which does not meet the Enlightenment's
empirical test for truth – must either be removed ("Christian" rationalism) or it must be recognized as myth and reinterpreted ("Christian" existentialism). And that, as Athanasius so emphatically
warned, leaves no room in the inn for Jesus Christ.

THE JESUS SEMINAR
In 1985, a group of scholars calling themselves Fellows of the
Jesus Seminar initiated a project to authenticate the words of Jesus
that are recorded in Scripture.[1] Seminar participants collected all the

words that Scripture attributes to Jesus, passed out colored beads to each member of the group, and conducted a poll to determine if group members believed that Jesus was the source of a particular saying. A red bead meant that Jesus definitely made the statement. A black bead indicated that Jesus definitely did not make the statement. A pink bead said that Jesus may have said it, and a gray bead meant that Jesus probably did not say it.

The Jesus Seminar concluded that 82 percent of the words ascribed to Jesus in the Gospels, including all words that indicate a divine origin or purpose for his life, were not actually spoken by him. They found no words of Jesus in the Gospel of John.

Jesus Seminar scholars conducted their research based on the controlling assumption that Jesus was something like a Jewish Socrates, one of many peripatetic teachers who traveled the Palestinian region at that time. They do not hesitate to affirm that his wisdom made an impact on the world, but they insist that human sagacity is the most that can be ascribed to him, and that Jesus himself never claimed powers greater than this. The idea that Jesus was divine, they argue, was credited to Jesus by his followers.

DEMYTHOLOGIZING THE SCRIPTURES

Scholarly bead counting is not new. None of the Jesus Seminar's presuppositions or conclusions is original. Its assumptions reflect the thought of Rudolf Bultmann (1884-1976), a post-Enlightenment theologian whose work constitutes a twentieth-century version of the Arian heresy. Bultmann sought to separate fact and myth in the New Testament narratives. What was really important, argued Bultmann, was *Jesus' symbolic meaning*, not the myriad of unproved and unprovable tales that fill the pages of Scripture.

In a lecture series delivered at Yale Divinity School in 1951, Bultmann stated his case: "The whole conception of the world which is presupposed in the preaching of Jesus as in the New Testament generally is mythological ... it is different from the conception of the world which has been formed and developed by science ... Modern science does not believe that the course of nature can be interrupted or, so to speak, perforated by supernatural powers."[2]

Pursuing that Enlightenment presupposition, Bultmann argues that the Jesus who is portrayed by the New Testament, "a great, preexistent heavenly being who became man for the sake of our redemption and took on himself suffering, even the suffering of the cross,"[3] is clearly a mythological figure, and as such he cannot relate meaningfully to moderns. With dogmatic certainty, Bultmann declares: "For modern man, the mythological conception of the world, the conceptions of eschatology, of redeemer and of redemption, are over and done with."[4]

Bultmann points out that the social gospel movement dealt with the problem by ignoring all mythological reference to Jesus and focusing on his ethical teachings. But, he says, that is not our only option. Another approach is to recognize that the mythological sayings of Jesus and about Jesus are a cover for some deeper meaning, a meaning that, once revealed, can offer a real moment of grace for modern humankind. To get to that meaning, one must demythologize the Gospel, *a process in which one supplies different meanings to its mythological symbols.*

Bultmann readily admits that any interpretation of the Gospel must employ a set of presuppositions, and he identifies his as being rooted in existentialist philosophy, particularly as he finds it in the work of Martin Heidegger. "Every interpreter is inescapably dependent on conceptions which he has inherited from a tradition ... and every tradition is dependent on some philosophy or other ... Our question is simply which philosophy today offers the most adequate perspective and conceptions for understanding human existence. Here it seems to me that we should learn from existentialist philosophy ..."[5]

Human beings cannot know anything, argues Bultmann, other than what they experience when they act or are acted upon. We can say nothing meaningful about God outside our own experience. Thus universal statements about God that speak of God as "eternal truth," for example, are meaningless. Bultmann says:

> Only such statements about God are legitimate as express the existential relations between God and man ... Statements which speak of God's actions as cosmic events are illegitimate. The affirmation that God is creator cannot be a theoretical statement about God as *creator mundi* in a general sense. The

> affirmation can only be a personal confession that I
> understand myself to be a creature which owes its
> existence to God ... Moreover, statements which
> describe God's action as cultic action, for example,
> that He offered His Son as a sacrificial victim, are
> not legitimate, unless they are understood in a pure-
> ly symbolic sense ...[6]

In the end, Bultmann is able to say that Jesus of Nazareth was a
historical character. But he labels "unscientific" any description of
Jesus as God Incarnate, and he rejects as implausible any notion of a
bodily resurrection. Incarnation, atonement, and resurrection have
meaning only in a symbolic sense, only in the sense that we experience them when we experience an existential encounter with the
Word of God. We can believe in God as creator only in the sense
that, when we are confronted by the Christ through God's Word, we
come to life in that existential encounter. We can believe in the resurrection only in the sense that, when we are confronted by God's
Word, our existence is affirmed over against that dreadful abyss that
threatens human beings with meaninglessness and death.

Bultmann puts it this way:

> God meets us in His Word, in a concrete word, the
> preaching instituted in Jesus Christ ... Accordingly
> it must be said that the Word of God is what it is
> only in the moment in which it is spoken. The Word
> of God is not a timeless statement but a concrete
> word addressed to men here and now ...[7]

Rudolf Bultmann's dependence on existentialist philosophy suggests an interesting parallel with Arius' dependence upon the notions
of Greek philosophers. Both men operated on the basis of a dualistic
assumption that God is unknowable, and that Jesus as an intermediary between God and humankind must be a representative creature.
Both Bultmann and Arius can speak of a *Christ concept*, one whose
impact on our experience engenders thoughts of a transcendent reality. But neither can ascribe to the Son the affirmation that is made by
Scripture, namely, that in Jesus Christ the fullness of God is present.

BULTMANN'S IMPACT ON THE MODERN CHURCH

The impact of Bultmann's methodology on the modern Church cannot be underestimated. In Europe, the practice of demythologizing Scripture became commonplace, and confidence in Scripture as a medium of divine revelation plummeted. That loss left the Church vulnerable to other Enlightenment notions, particularly the dogma that there is no eternal truth. The truth was replaced with "truths," attested to by individuals from their own personal experiences.

Having discarded Scripture's authoritative voice, the Church had no basis on which to counter relativism's claims. Pitting one person's experience against another proved an unfruitful exercise (who can challenge what another person "feels"?), leading to the balkanization of the Christian community into multiple enclaves of individual opinion.

Europe's cathedrals that tower over every major city and whose village churches attest to their once-central role in community life, soon became ecclesiastical museums, ceremonial establishments that legitimize culture with empty ritual. Bultmann, and other writers in both Church and culture who accepted his premises, had introduced Europe to a very different Jesus – Arius' Jesus – and the Word-made-flesh departed, leaving fossilized relics of a once-lively faith.

AMERICA FOLLOWS SUIT

Theologians in the United States were slow to accept Bultmann's thesis. Inviting people into a personal relationship with Jesus Christ, American Protestantism in the early twentieth century experienced revival and periods of robust growth. Well into the 1950s, as Bultmann's teaching career in Marburg was coming to an end, the Churches of America showed signs of vitality. Soaring statistics documented the fact that this was boom time for America's congregations. Sanctuaries and fellowship halls were under construction everywhere. Conference centers drew record crowds. Financial contributions poured into denominational coffers.

During this period, the country's prestigious Protestant seminaries dedicated themselves to biblical and doctrinal studies. The Presbyterian Church's premier seminaries, Princeton Theological Seminary, serving primarily the Northern stream, and Union Theological Seminary in Virginia, serving the South, maintained a strong emphasis on Scripture and doctrine. Charles Hodge and B.B. Warfield had bequeathed to Princeton a commitment to the authority of Scripture that stood it in good stead for many years.

Union Theological Seminary attracted a faculty of renowned biblical scholars. Union's John Bright and James Mays commanded the field in Old Testament studies, their books serving as texts for Protestant seminaries throughout the world. Balmer Kelly won similar respect among New Testament scholars in the United States. John Leith was accorded critical acclaim for his work in doctrinal theology, his volumes on Christian doctrine gaining widespread acceptance as definitive texts. *Interpretation*, a prestigious journal of Bible and theology, was founded on Union Seminary's campus and became a benchmark for modern biblical studies.

Students who grew under such tutelage were expected to achieve excellence in the preaching and teaching of God's word. The emphasis of a theological education was on substance, not methodology. Ministerial candidates were examined for their exegetical competence in the Word, and they were tested for their knowledge of the Church's doctrinal history. It was deemed important that they know what happened at Nicaea, that they understand the implications of that fourth-century debate, and that they could recognize an Arian Jesus when he appeared in modern clothing.

As biblical and doctrinal scholars of international stature retired from America's Protestant seminary faculties, they were replaced by a new breed of academics. Spawned by the modernist-fundamentalist disputes of the 1920s that prompted J. Gresham Machen and several other faculty members to leave Princeton and found Westminster Theological Seminary, the new breed entertained a passion for liberation. God was to be discovered in *praxis*. Theology would rise from the bottom, from base camps of human experience.

The operative word for the new enthusiasts was relevance. They wanted for contemporary theology that congruence with modern worldviews that Bultmann had articulated in Europe. For too long, they argued, the Church has set the world's agenda. From now on, the world will set the Church's agenda. The Church must proclaim a secular Gospel for a secular world. Bishop John A.T. Robinson's *Honest to God*, Harvey Cox's *Secular City*, John Hick's *Myth of God Incarnate*, and numerous study papers from mainline denominational bureaucracies reflect this transition from belief that is rooted in revealed truth to beliefs that arise from human reflections upon secular events.

UNION THEOLOGICAL SEMINARY IN VIRGINIA

Although almost any mainline denominational seminary in the United States offers evidence of Bultmann's influence,[8] few exhibit so dramatic a turn as that which has occurred at Union Theological Seminary in Virginia. After almost two decades of declining influence on the American theological scene – occasioned, its critics argue, by the administration's replacing retiring world-renowned biblical/confessional theologians with proponents of post-Enlightenment modernism – open conflict has broken out within the seminary's faculty.

In the center of that struggle stand two of the seminary's tenured professors, Douglas F. Ottati, and Jack D. Kingsbury. Under the influence of Ottati, who has enjoyed the full support and encouragement of the institution's president, Union Theological Seminary has undergone a dramatic shift. One need not go all the way to Nicaea to meet the Arian Christ, for he appears throughout the themes of Ottati's theology.

At a meeting of the seminary's Board of Trustees on February 17, 1995, Kingsbury, Professor of Biblical Theology, went public with his concern over the institution's theological drift. He took issue with Ottati's theology as it is articulated in his book *Jesus Christ and Christian Vision*.[9] That book, said Kingsbury, includes views on the authority of Scripture and the atonement and resurrection of Jesus Christ that depart radically from the Reformed tradition.

JESUS CHRIST AND CHRISTIAN VISION

Douglas Ottati says that his purpose in writing *Jesus Christ and Christian Vision* is to "present a christology of the heart that is *informed* by the classical Christian heritage and engages contemporary believers."[10] He holds that there is "continuity" between the Jesus of history and the figure of Jesus Christ as portrayed by the New Testament writers.[11] At the same time, he claims that "much of what the New Testament portrays as historical occurrence actually amounts to narrative and *symbolic thematization* that aims to display the meaning of Jesus Christ for early Christian communities."[12] In the New Testament, says Ottati, Jesus Christ becomes a "symbolic form," or pattern.[13] As a symbolic form, Jesus Christ indicates how the Christian community is to comprehend God and human life in responsive relation to God.[14]

JESUS CHRIST: A "SYMBOLIC FORM"

Ottati's reference to Jesus Christ as a "symbolic form" is significant, as when, for example, he addresses the question of the divinity of Jesus Christ. He says that the Chalcedonian Definition of 451 that "Jesus Christ is actually God and actually man" is a flawed doctrine, poetry changed into dogma.[15] For Ottati, "Jesus Christ is a mundane medium of revelation."[16] What we find in him is a person whose heart and life are oriented by a dominant devotion to God.[17] In this sense, Jesus Christ may be depicted as "the brightest *illustration* of grace" or of a "God-shaped *man*."[18]

So did God become incarnate in Jesus Christ? Ottati gives no direct answer. He suggests that Jesus is "supreme," and he calls Jesus a "manifestation of God," but he avoids making any ontological distinction that would differentiate Jesus Christ from other humans, who are also manifestations of God. The reader is left to wonder if Ottati can agree with Nicaea that Jesus Christ is "Very God ... being of one substance with the Father," for that is precisely the language that he insists must be avoided.

PHYSICAL RESURRECTION UNNECESSARY

On the question of Jesus' resurrection, Ottati admits that his interpretation will not be much help for the preacher at Easter.[19] What counted for the New Testament Church, Ottati claims, is not whether God raised Jesus physically from the dead, but whether the early Christians "*had experiences* of the continuing presence of Christ after his crucifixion."[20] Referring to Scripture's statement, "He is risen," Ottati says only that the primary importance of that confession for the early Christians was that Jesus Christ was "the risen Lord of their continuing experience."[21] Ottati nowhere affirms the objective, personal reality of the risen, crucified Christ whom the disciples recognized, heard, and touched, with whom they dined, and by whom they were commissioned to evangelize the world.

In response to a growing chorus of Presbyterian ministers who have, in fact, found little in his theology that will preach on Easter Sunday, Ottati offered further comments in a *Presbyterian Outlook* article titled "Meditation on Easter Sunday."[22] He said that Jesus' resurrection is God's "yes" to a God-initiated, loving way of living. "The resurrection vindicates Jesus' ministry of reconciliation and it calls us to follow," he said. But when one asks what actually happened on Easter morning, Ottati shies away from anything that might be called physical. "I do not believe that the chief meaning of Jesus' resurrection is a matter of elusive physics or metaphysics," he said. "You may have been told when you were younger that unless you believe that bodies come back to life, you're not saved ... But don't you believe it." The important thing about the resurrection, he said, is "the grace of God" and the fact that "the point of your life is new life and true life."

Old Testament scholar James Mays responded to Ottati's article: "First, the resurrection of Jesus should not be reduced to a 'meaning.' The term (noun and verb) is a favorite and elusive device used by some theologians to shift attention from subject to significance. It is used ten times in the article and is said to be the truly important thing about the resurrection of Jesus.

"Second, the resurrection of Jesus must be dealt with as an event. The uncertainty of its 'physics' is not the issue. The issue is the objective historicity of the event referred to by 'resurrection of Jesus.' A responsible case for the historical reliability of the traditions of the appearances of Jesus and of the empty tomb can be made.

"Third, the resurrection of Jesus must not be conceived as an event that happened only in the consciousness of the disciples. That 'God raised Jesus from the dead' refers to the basis and object of the disciples' faith and not just their faith ..."[23]

REINVENTING THE CREEDS

In "My Christology," a paper Ottati distributed on Union's campus in 1995, he claims that he stands with the Nicene Creed of 325 and the Chalcedonian Definition of 451 in their affirmation of "the centrality of Jesus Christ." Professor Kingsbury charges, however, that Ottati misrepresents the creeds. The question at Nicaea and

Chalcedon, says Kingsbury, "was not merely 'Is Jesus Christ central?' but 'In what sense is he God?' " Ottati's version of Nicaea and Chalcedon, says Kingsbury, falls fatally short of what those documents and creeds actually confess.

Kingsbury points out that Ottati can tell us that Jesus Christ is a symbol, a teacher, an exemplar, an illustration, and a guide. Just as Arius did at Nicaea, he can even use "Son of God" as an honorific title as long as it has no ontological significance. But what Ottati does not say – in fact, what he steadfastly refuses to say – is that in Jesus Christ, God became incarnate, that Jesus died on the cross as the all-sufficient salvation for all people, and that God raised Jesus from the grave as God's final victory over death.

THE SINFUL CHRIST

Ottati finds the idea that Jesus Christ was without sin entirely unnecessary and, in fact, unpalatable. "For a number of reasons, which I explain in some detail on pp. 109-114 of *Jesus Christ and Christian Vision*, I neither believe it necessary or appropriate to uphold most classical notions of Jesus' sinless perfection."[24]

In answer to colleagues who have reminded Ottati that Scripture, particularly the book of Hebrews, describes Jesus Christ as sinless, Ottati argues in his book that there is plenty of scriptural evidence that Jesus was "in the grip of passionate conflicts," and in his paper Ottati says he just doesn't agree with Hebrews 4:15. He argues that the Gospel portraits of Jesus present a man who is affected by Jewish prejudice toward Gentiles, who experiences temptations in the wilderness, who resists the cross while praying in the garden of Gethsemane, and who expresses doubt on the cross. He says that Jesus' "dominant devotion" to God's will remained in place, but that within that affection, there is plenty of room for a very human, human being. He also says that the Gospel of Matthew portrays a Jesus who "grows in his vision of what is required by his dominant devotion," indicating that Jesus made improvements in pursuit of his dominant devotion as he matured.[25]

Ottati has no trouble quoting the first part of Hebrews 4:15: "For we have not a high priest who is unable to sympathize with our weaknesses, but one who in every respect has been tempted as we are," but he balks on the final phrase of that verse, "yet without sinning." At that point Ottati flatly denies the scriptural affirmation: "When I say that it is not necessary or appropriate to insist on Jesus' sinless perfection, I do in fact depart from Hebrews ..."[26]

ROSEMARY RADFORD RUETHER

Part of Union Theological Seminary's growing public relations problem with the Presbyterian Church (USA) lies in the fact that its faculty invited Rosemary Radford Ruether to deliver its prestigious James Sprunt lectures. (Professor Ottati chaired the faculty committee that recommended the appointment.) Ruether is one of the most prominent radical feminist leaders in the church today. A professor of applied theology at Garrett-Evangelical Theological Seminary, she is an acknowledged leader in a movement designed to rid the Christian tradition of its "patriarchy," the sin of male dominance over women.

Ruether's efforts represent a great deal more than a societal attempt to overcome inequities between males and females in the marketplace. The crux of that problem, she argues, lies in theology. God, for Ruether, is essentially a projection of the human imagination, a concept of culture. Ruether finds the God whom Christians have traditionally worshiped inadequate because, she asserts, this God was created by a culture of patriarchal males. She suggests that the time has come to create another God(dess), one more acceptable to the experience of women.

REVELATION VS. "REVELATORY EXPERIENCE"

In existential fashion, Ruether says that all theology begins with a "revelatory experience." Her theology is not dependent on the existence of a deity in any objective or ontological sense: A person's *subjective experience* of some extraordinary dimension to life will suffice. In fact, she defines revelation, which Scripture calls an act of God, in purely human terms. In a theological oxymoron, Ruether says that revelation is a human act. "We must postulate that every great religious idea begins in the revelatory experience. By *revelatory* we mean breakthrough experiences beyond ordinary fragmented consciousness that provide interpretive symbols illuminating the means of the *whole* of life. Since consciousness is ultimately individual, we postulate that revelation always starts with an individual."[27]

In Ruether's definition of revelation, the influence of Descartes, Kant, Kierkegaard, Bultmann and others becomes transparent. Ruether is unable to ascribe substance to anything outside the self, affirming that all she can truly know is her own experience. This is the epistemological starting point for her radical feminism.

Religion, for Ruether, is a way of interpreting one's experience, a paradigm for making sense out of our sensations. If an individual's religious idea becomes contagious and grows to become a group's idea, then clusters of ritual and tradition are formed around it. A community is born, made up of people who share a common perspective. Both their history and their interpretation of present events are filtered through this common lens.

In time they codify their interpretation in writings, and they declare these documents sacred. They develop institutions and offices whose function is to refer all matters to the sacred writings for an authoritative interpretation. They develop a system of discipline wherein they can identify and "marginalize" any members of the community who fail to adhere to the correct interpretation of the original divine revelation.[28]

PATRIARCHY

Ruether's complaint is that for centuries, male "revelatory experiences" have been normative, and males have controlled the institutions that determine and enforce orthodoxy. Females have been forced to worship gods conceived by males and to accept salvation from the son of a male God. Her solution to the problem is to introduce other divinities into the mix, goddesses who emerge from the female experience.

Ruether appreciates Jesus of Nazareth insofar as he was a prophetic liberator who promoted radical egalitarianism, but she has no use for him as a divine human being and as the medium of our salvation.[29] Ruether believes that the Jesus described in Scripture is an aberration of the historical Jesus. She believes that his followers diverted his ministry from its liberating course when they endured "the shock of the Crucifixion" and proceeded to fabricate the story of his resurrection in order to make the whole thing come out right. This then led to the formation of a community that worshiped the male Jesus Christ and developed patriarchal traditions and structures.

Jesus of Nazareth, the human liberator whose *ideas* were divine, i.e., filled with breakthrough experiences that are "beyond ordinary fragmented consciousness," was transfigured by male New Testament writers into Jesus Christ, the divine Savior. Scriptures were developed to codify this interpretation. Clergy was ordained to enforce orthodoxy by referencing all new ideas to the benchmark of Scripture. By the time bishops entered the picture, the possibility of recognizing any further revelation was closed.[30] With the development of an organizational structure and Christian clergy, says Ruether, the marginalization of the female was complete: "The possession of male genitalia becomes the essential prerequisite for representing Christ, who is the disclosure of the male God."[31]

THE GOSPEL OF LIBERATION

Ruether believes that when Jesus of Nazareth announced his egalitarian message, he transcended his maleness. He was speaking as one who himself had been redeemed by the Gospel of egalitarianism. It was precisely because he had been liberated from patriarchy that he could be the instrument to liberate others. Ruether refers to "Jesus as the Christ" in contrast to Jesus of Nazareth when she wishes to emphasize his liberating, i.e., "divine," role. "In this sense Jesus as the Christ, the representative of liberated humanity and the liberating Word of God, manifests the *kenosis of patriarchy,* the announcement of the new humanity through a lifestyle that discards hierarchical caste privilege and speaks on behalf of the lowly."[32]

Ruether's Jesus is thus reduced to a symbol of human possibility. Just as Jesus the man was liberated from patriarchy, so others can be led to that same liberation. And Jesus is the one to do it since he himself experienced it. He is "divine" only in the sense that he has become the bearer of the divine liberating word. "Christ, as redemptive person, and Word of God, is not to be encapsulated 'once-and-for-all' in the historical Jesus. The Christian community continues Christ's identity ... Christ, the liberated humanity, is not confined to a static perfection of one person two thousand years ago. Rather, redemptive humanity goes ahead of us, calling us to yet incomplete dimensions of human liberation."[33]

Ruether's Christ bears a remarkable resemblance to the Christ whom Douglas Ottati describes as a "symbolic form." Both Ruether and Ottati echo Bultmann's complaint that the Jesus Christ of Scripture is largely a creation of the early Church, a historical figure whose vision of God and ethical teachings got him crucified, and who was then mythologized by his followers.

THE SON DISAPPEARS OVER THE HORIZON

Ruether's Christ has not been limited to academia. In 1994, Presbyterian Women, the national women's organization in the Presbyterian Church (USA) marketed a "Horizons Bible Study" among local women's groups throughout the denomination. Written by R. David Kaylor, who notes that his trips with student groups to India and Central America "have led him to look at the Bible with fresh eyes," the study treats the New Testament epistles as products of first-century sociologists rather than the result of God's revelation. Notable in the study is the distinction that Kaylor makes between the human Jesus and the divine Christ. In lieu of an affirmation that Scripture is the unique and authoritative witness to Jesus Christ, the study consistently lifts the primacy of individual experience over the witness of Scripture as a guide to faith and life. In lieu of affirming the Christian faith as expressed historically in the Nicene and Apostles' Creeds, the study relies on a class struggle anthropology.

The 1994 Horizons Bible Study was reviewed and found wanting by leaders of many Presbyterian congregations. Speaking for the Session's Nurture Committee at First Presbyterian Church in Baton Rouge, Louisiana, Lloyd Lunceford announced his committee's analysis of Kaylor's work: "Reformed theology ... has always held that Jesus of Nazareth was both fully God and fully man. [e.g., 'very God of very God,' 'true God and true Man,' 'two whole, perfect, and distinct natures, the Godhead and the manhood, were inseparably joined together in one person.'] The author, however, establishes a dichotomy between the humanity of Jesus of Nazareth and the deity of the pre- and post-incarnate Christ. Notably absent was any clear statement of Jesus of Nazareth as fully God in bodily form (echoing strains of second and fourth-century Gnosticism and Arianism)."[34]

This Bible Study and the fact that national leaders of the Presbyterian Women organization participated in and wholly endorsed the Re-Imagining conference, have triggered a resistance movement against their national church leaders by local Presbyterian Women groups. Since 1993, contributions to the national treasury of Presbyterian Women and the use of its study materials have declined substantially, according to triennial reports made by the group's leaders to its membership.

NOTHING NEW UNDER THE SUN

Our review of the Nicene debates reminds us that there is nothing particularly new in the themes that Ruether, Ottati and others are promoting in the Church today. Theirs is a variation on the theme that Arius argued many centuries ago. What Ruether and Ottati have promoted in the name of the Gospel is not theology (literally, "a word about God"), but a blend of sociology and politics. Theologian Alan Lewis properly identified the problem when in a review of Ottati's book he said, "Nothing happens from God's side in the life of [Ottati's] Jesus."[35]

NOTES

1. The results of their work have been published in *The Five Gospels: The Search for the Authentic Words of Jesus,* by Robert Funk, et. al., (New York: Macmillan Publishing Co., 1993).
2. Rudolf Bultmann, *Jesus Christ and Mythology* (New York: Charles Scribner's Sons, 1958), p. 15.
3. Ibid., p. 16.
4. Ibid.
5. Ibid., p. 55.
6. Ibid., p. 69.
7. Ibid., p. 78.
8. Readers are encouraged to read Thomas Oden's *Requiem* (Nashville: Abingdon Press, 1995) for a recent critique of U.S. mainline seminaries. Oden is a member of the United Methodist Church and holds a tenured position on the faculty of the Theological School at Drew University.
9. Douglas F. Ottati, *Jesus Christ and Christian Vision* (Minneapolis: Fortress Press, 1989).
10. Ibid., p. vii, emphasis added.
11. Ibid., p. 69.
12. Ibid., emphasis added.
13. Ibid., pp. 50, 69.
14. Ibid.
15. Ibid., pp. 96-97.
16. Ibid., p. 101.
17. Ibid., p. 99.
18. Ibid., p. 100, emphasis added.
19. Ibid., p. 93.
20. Ibid., p. 94, emphasis added.
21. Ibid., p. 94.
22. Douglas Ottati, "Meditation on Easter Sunday," in *The Presbyterian Outlook*, April 1, 1996, pp. 5-7.
23. James Mays, "Comments on the Resurrection," in *The Presbyterian Outlook*, April 22-29, 1996, p. 2.
24. "My Christology," a paper distributed by Douglas Ottati to members of the Union Theological Seminary community, p. 16.

25. Ottati, *Jesus Christ and Christian Vision*, p. 109-115.
26. Ottati, *My Christology*, p. 16.
27. Rosemary Radford Ruether, *Sexism and God-Talk* (Boston: Beacon Press, 1983), p. 13.
28. Ibid., p. 13-14.
29. Ibid., pp. 114-115.
30. Ibid., pp. 122-123.
31. Ibid., p. 126.
32. Ibid., p. 137.
33. Ibid., p. 138.
34. Report of the First Presbyterian Church Nurture Committee, Baton Rouge, Louisiana, May 25, 1994.
35. Review of *Jesus Christ and Christian Vision* by Alan E. Lewis in *The Presbyterian Outlook*, March 26, 1990, pp. 13-14.

PART FOUR

SIGNS OF HOPE

On this rock I will build My Church.
                                    Matthew 16:18

*I am the Alpha and the Omega, the Beginning and
the End, the First and the Last.*
                                    Revelation 22:13

Like our ancestors at Nicaea, we are engaged in the thick of a battle for the soul of the Church. Post-Enlightenment ideologues continue to control denominational structures, but the ships that they captain are quickly losing momentum. Indeed, they are foundering in stormy seas. The fact of the storm itself is a sign of hope, for it means that Christians are unwilling to support a witness that is not faithful to the Gospel.

Other signs abound. New witnesses are stepping forward, challenging the dualistic presuppositions of a dying culture. They are not ashamed of the Gospel. In numerous local faith communities, a once-moribund Church is springing to life in fresh and vital ministries both at home and abroad.

Ignored by a generation of Church leaders, the lessons of Nicaea are again being learned by Christians who have found untenable the promises of post-Enlightenment optimism. Invigorated by studies in Scripture and Christian doctrine, the people of the Church are renewing their conversation with the Lord of the Church. In doing so, they are discovering the rock on which the Church was built, and the gates of Hell will not prevail against it.

13

STANDING FIRM

If you do not stand firm,
Surely you will not be stood firm.

Isaiah 7:9b*

Mainline denominations in the United States are in trouble.[1] Membership losses over the past three decades have been staggering. Objecting to their leaders' accommodation to secularism, thousands of congregations are reducing or eliminating financial support for national ecclesiastical structures. But denominational officials show no signs of abandoning their course. Like the former Soviet regime that blamed decades of agricultural deficits on bad weather, these officials will not admit publicly that the losses relate to their leadership. Instead, they blame superficialities like demographics. In each of more than twenty annual reports to this denomination's General Assemblies, Presbyterian leaders have announced their belief that the trend has bottomed out.

But if the cause of mainline decline is demographic, how does one explain the fact that in the place and time that denominations are dying, evangelical groups are growing at an unprecedented rate? The issue has little to do with sociology. It has everything to do with Christian faith.

Rev. Herbert Valentine, a recent moderator of the Presbyterian Church (USA) General Assembly, ascribes congregational opposition to national church policies to a desire for certainty. Modern

*Author's translation

society and the modern Church are confronted by changing times, he said to a 1996 forum for Presbyterian officials.[2] "These are apocalyptic ... chaotic ... paradigm shifting ... wilderness ... kairos times." In such times, Valentine said, "three scary demons come out to intimidate us: frustration, depression, and paralysis." The denominational leader warned Presbyterians to beware of those who would lure the masses with siren songs of certainty. Certainty in matters of faith, he said in a speech that could have been scripted by Descartes, is not the answer. Instead, Valentine suggested, one must learn to celebrate life's ambiguities.

Valentine compared the mainline denomination's crisis to problems experienced by the Israelites during the Exodus. He reminded his audience that when the children of Israel faced their wilderness uncertainties, they, too, turned against their leaders. They demanded that they be returned to Egypt, a romanticized Egypt that never existed. He asserted that Israel found its answer, not in an elusive search for certainty, but in the wilderness itself. For Valentine and other celebrants of ambiguity, there was no crossing of the Jordan, no assurance of a promised land: "Look toward the wilderness," he urged his fellow Presbyterians.

SEARCHING FOR CERTAINTY

Valentine's diagnosis contains a touch of truth. People *are* looking for certainty today. That search is part of what it means to be human. Augustine got it right when he prayed to the only reality that can give us confidence, "Thou hast made us for thyself, O Lord, and our hearts are restless till they find their rest in Thee."[3]

But rapid change is not the culprit, for every age has been faced with changing circumstances. As horrible as it may be, AIDS is no more ravaging than was the bubonic plague, or the potato famine, or the Holocaust. Quantum physics is no less an intellectual challenge today than were Galileo's observations to those who thought the Earth was the center of the universe. Human beings in every age have adapted to changing circumstances and shifting paradigms. The problem is not change per se, but the abandonment of belief in the One whose presence offers confidence in the midst of change. While justly criticizing the Israelites for romanticizing their past, Valentine romanticizes the present. He has traded one idol for another.

The superficiality of such a diagnosis explains the impotency of its prescription. The Israelites found strength, not in looking "*toward the wilderness*," but in looking *through* it. Moses knew what post-Enlightenment thinkers cannot comprehend: Matter is not all that matters. Wilderness is not the whole story. It is the stage on which the story is told.

Seeking certainty in the midst of their wanderings, the Israelites melted trinkets and molded their own gods, the ancient idolatry that today's Re-Imaginers would have us repeat. Assuming that nothing can be known beyond what one can touch and feel, they fashioned deities from the stuff of their own experience. But homemade deities offer no confidence and no basis for community. They merely baptize our fragmentation. Scripture says, "In those days there was no king in Israel; everyone did what was right in his own eyes."[4] This picture of an association of atomized individuals, each pandering to his or her own homemade god, is strikingly modern.

REVELATION AND COMMUNITY

It was in the wilderness that the God who refuses to be named[5] revealed himself. Here the Israelites encountered their deliverer: "I am the Lord your God, who brought you out ... of the house of bondage. You shall have no other Gods before me."[6] It was to be in communion with this God that they would be reconstituted as a people. No longer would they be merely a collection of fugitives. "Once you were no people," declared Peter, "now you are God's people."[7]

Revelation, God's self-disclosure amidst our wilderness wanderings, gives us the *certainty* that we seek. The Gospel of John announced it: "The Word became flesh and dwelt among us, full of grace and truth; we have beheld his glory, glory as of the only Son from the Father."[8]

Revelation also gives us the *community* we seek. When Peter – moved not by reason but by revelation – said of Jesus, "You are the Christ, the Son of the Living God," Jesus responded, "Blessed are you, Simon Bar-Jonah, for flesh and blood has not revealed this to you, but My Father who is in heaven ... on this rock I will build My Church, and the gates of Hell shall not prevail against it."[9] This is the basis of Christian certainty, and it is because we have this certainty that we also have hope.

THE SUBSTANCE OF HOPE

Hope is a powerful word. For the Christian, it means far more than a wish, for a wish is merely a desire. We wish for what we do not have, usually without any basis for expecting that we shall receive it. Wishes look toward the future. Hope, on the other hand, looks both ways. Unlike a wish, Christian hope is grounded in a past event, a historical reality. Hope justifies a future expectation based on something that has already happened. Hebrews voices this past/present dimension: "Now faith is the *substance* of things hoped for, the *evidence* of things not seen."[10]

Therefore, when one looks for signs of hope in the Church today, one must begin at the beginning. The foundation of the Church is Jesus Christ. He is both the pioneer and the perfecter of our faith, the one from whom we came and to whom we go. He is the Son of God, of the same essence as the Father. He announces the presence of that divine community of persons-in-relation, the Trinity, that creates, redeems and sustains us. The future of the Church, then, is not dependent on our faithfulness, wisdom or eloquence. The Church is the body of Christ, the one whom death could not destroy. Secure in Christ's promise, the Church will never die.

This is not to say that every institutional expression of the Church is invincible. In fact, those ecclesiastical institutions that deny the foundational truths of the Christian faith are dying. Trans-fusions from the financial investments of a once-vital faith may carry them for a season, but unless they return to the truth, death is imminent. If that happens, Jesus Christ will not be left without a wit-ness. History reminds us that when ecclesiastical institutions fail him, others rise to take their place.

FIGHT OR FLIGHT: A CHOICE FOR MAINLINE CHURCH EVANGELICALS

So what are evangelical members of mainline churches to do? Shall we shake the dust from our feet and depart for communions more amenable to Christian truth? Shall we abandon a sinking ship?

Athanasius stood firm. He refused to leave. In fact, as hard as they tried, ecclesiastical officials could not throw him out. It is instructive to remember that he spent 20 of his 45 years as a bishop in exile, that he was a fugitive, and that at one point in his career, all Church councils – both in the East and in the West – rejected him.

One cannot read his correspondence during that period without sensing the terrible discouragement that he experienced with each of his defeats. But it is also true that even when officialdom did its worst, Athanasius was never alone. He lived with the conviction that the Lord whom he loved would not abandon him, and he discovered thousands of witnesses who never bowed their knees to Baal. Pursued many times by magistrates, soldiers, and ecclesiastical functionaries, Athanasius always managed to escape. When adversity struck, faithful Christian communities stepped forward to hide, feed and nurture him, even at the risk of their own lives. Athanasius never left the Church, and the Church – in spite of what was done by its officials – did not leave him. His obligation was to stand firm in the place where God had placed him, and he proved faithful to that call.

One shudders to speculate on the consequences had Athanasius caved in to Arius' aberrations. The Church of all ages owes a great debt to this man who publicly challenged the heresy of his time and stood firm amidst the maelstrom that his witness unleashed. Resisting an establishment that compromises its integrity has never been popular. There is a price to be paid for faithfulness. But there is also a reward, for people of resurrection faith know that the truth can be buried only for a season. We are called to give a faithful witness to the Gospel in whatever arena God has placed us. Our local congregations constitute such an arena, and abandonment is not an option. We must stay until our task is done.

The Presbyterian Lay Committee, a reform organization working within the Presbyterian Church (USA), is often contacted by evangelicals who are tempted to give up on the denomination. The argument that conservatives most frequently proffer is that they are weary of fighting church leaders who preach a false gospel. Better, they say, to invest one's time, money and talents in the Lord's great commission, proclaiming the Gospel throughout the world. "What we need to be doing," they say, "is evangelism and missions."

Worldwide missions is a worthy enterprise, one that every Christian should support. To be sure, there is a romantic aura that surrounds the idea of taking the Gospel to far away heathens. But what about that mission field on our doorstep? Evangelicals should not look on theological controversy as an annoyance to be avoided. Rather, this debate offers a golden opportunity for evangelism. Mission includes being faithful witnesses to our own church institutions among people who, often unawares, follow a counterfeit Christ. Not only for the Church's integrity, but for the sake of their own souls, they must learn to identify the Arian impostor and turn to the only Christ who will save.

In *The God Who Is There*, Francis Schaeffer describes the descent of post-Enlightenment humanity beneath the line of despair. Those who live above the line affirm the existence of absolutes, and they order their lives accordingly. But modern culture has increasingly moved below the line, into nihilistic relativism. Below the line residents claim tolerance as their highest virtue, and they profess to live on the basis of an all-ideas-are-equal assumption. Schaeffer points out, however, that proponents of this ideology do not practice what they preach. They cannot do so, for the logical extension of their professed point of view is suicide. One cannot eat, work, or associate in community without making choices, and choices presuppose the existence of absolutes.

In fact, therefore, although people below the line of despair say they do not believe in absolutes, they act as if they do. With every choice we make, we are affirming the existence of some criteria, some standard, on which the choice was made. Every time we recoil at the news of an atrocity, we acknowledge a sense of right and wrong. Thus, the nihilistic relativist is inconsistent, affirming an ideology that he cannot practice and remain alive on this planet.

Schaeffer says that this inconsistency is the point of contact for evangelism. The first task of the Christian is to push post-Enlightenment people to the logical conclusion of what they profess, forcing them to face the incompatibility between their ideology and their daily choices. Rather than beginning a conversation with the Gospel, Schaeffer encourages us to establish the neighbor's point of vulnerability:

> We try to move [the absolute relativist] in the natural direction in which his presuppositions would take him. We are then pushing him towards the place where he ought to be, had he not stopped short.[11]

Schaeffer warns us not to engage in this destructive activity as a game. It is serious business, and it will cause pain for those who discover the aridity of their presuppositions. The exercise would be cruel unless engaged by one who truly cares about the other person.

> The whole purpose of our speaking to twentieth-century people in this way is not to make them admit that we are right in some personally superior way, not to push their noses in the dirt, but to make them see their need so that they will listen to the Gospel. As soon as the man before us is ready to listen to the Gospel we do not push him any further, because it is horrible to be propelled in the direction of meaninglessness against the testimony of the external world and the testimony of oneself.[12]

HOMEWORK

Sharing the Gospel at home can be a messy and difficult task. Personal relationships and business and social factors can present complications in a culture that dismissively equates conviction with self-righteousness. It is easier to tell the story to strangers. And when our testimony is challenged, few of us feel that we are equipped to argue on behalf of the faith that is within us. That is a task – technically called apologetics – that not only our laypeople, but most of our clergy, feel incompetent to handle.

One of the more hopeful signs of reformation within the Presbyterian Church today is the emergence of the Charles Hodge Society, a student group on the campus of Princeton Theological Seminary. Naming its fellowship in honor of one of Princeton's premier nineteenth-century theologians, the Society devotes much of its attention to apologetics.

Once an essential component of classical theological education, courses in apologetics are rarely taught today in mainline seminaries. The notion of rational argument in defense of Christian truth crosses the grain of post-Enlightenment assumptions that equate faith with feeling. However, the consequence of dropping apologetics from seminary curricula has been a generation of ministers who have no idea how to defend the faith.[13]

Charles Hodge Society members believe that theology since the Enlightenment has been largely entrapped in sentiment, with faith described as a personal experience to be celebrated, not a truth subject to inquiry. While members of the society do not question Christianity's experiential dimension, they argue that the celebration of religious experience alone results in sloppy sentimentality. After all, they observe, religious experience points beyond itself. One has an experience of something or someone, and one's ideas about that reality can be tested.

The Society enhances students' theological preparation at Princeton Seminary by offering its own unofficial and not-for-credit apologetics seminar on campus. Immediately popular, the meetings drew an average of 30 students during its first year (1995). Participants were encouraged to try their hand at a written apologetic by choosing an attack on the Christian faith and then defending that aspect of the faith that has come under attack. The format includes: (1) select and state a concrete argument that has been advanced against the Christian faith, taking care to be precise and to avoid caricaturing the position. (2) Identify the argument's appeal and its strengths. (3) Specify how this argument undermines the Christian faith. (4) Refute the argument.

The return of apologetics to Princeton has stimulated considerable excitement, not only on the Princeton campus, but among student groups at other Presbyterian seminaries as well. Presbyterians across the country are becoming familiar with the work of the Charles Hodge Society through exposure to its journal, the *Princeton Theological Review*. These developments among future members of the Presbyterian clergy constitute a sign of hope for the Church.

REDISCOVERING THE BIBLE

Although institutional reorganization efforts (for the most part, "downsizing") are rampant among the mainline's national bureaucracies, it is difficult to discern any real reform. The story is quite different, however, at the congregational level. Here, Christians are increasingly coming together as nurturing communities in the face of a deep sense of estrangement from secular culture. Rejecting curricula produced by their denominational offices,[14] congregations are forming small groups to study the Bible. Church members are once again learning the language of biblical faith. In the context of those who share their faith, they are gaining confidence in their ability to articulate their Christian beliefs.

As they absorb and reinforce Christian culture in small group settings, church members are placing greater value on their congregations as communities of faith. Here they challenge the ideology of rationalism and relativism that dominates America's entertainment establishment, media establishment, government schools (no longer regarded as "public schools"), the arts, and politics. Encouraged by their faith communities, Christians are becoming more intentional about rearing their children in a Christian context, more selective in accessing media programming, more creative in designing alternatives or enhancements to government education, and more insistent on cutting off public funds for cultural enterprises that offend their Christian faith and morals.

The growth of these faith communities and the values they represent have not gone unnoticed by politicians. All political parties are developing strategies to exploit Christian objections to the cultural wasteland in which they live. While some forms of this exploitation constitute regrettable distortions, the fact that politicians have taken notice of Christian concerns indicates that such concerns are being articulated more frequently and effectively. The growth of congregational faith communities and their cumulative impact on secular culture constitute another sign of hope.

REDISCOVERING DOCTRINE

Bible study is crucial to the Church's reformation, and it is a matter of first priority for Christians. But it is not the only priority. We approach the Bible with presuppositions. We process what we read through filters of prior knowledge and personal proclivities. Thus, our reading can produce myriad understandings, all of which – because we are fallible – must be tested. It is important, therefore that Christians study the Scriptures in conversation with one another.

But our conversation must not be limited to present-tense partners. We claim membership in the "communion of the saints," that experience of the Church that transcends boundaries of time and space. When we celebrate the Lord's Supper, we do so amidst a great cloud of witnesses. At the table with us are Mary and Martha, Peter,

James and John, Alexander and Athanasius, Martin Luther and John Calvin, Charles Wesley and Charles Hodge, Christian brothers and sisters of the past, present and future. We belong to one another in that human community, made holy by its incorporation into a divine communion called Father, Son and Holy Spirit.

That is why the study of Christian doctrine is so important. It is crucial, for example, that Christians today know what happened in Nicaea, for in that place their forebears struggled through an important truth about the God in whom we all live and move and have our being. While nothing can substitute for our study of the Scriptures, that study must occur *in conversation with the whole Church*. The history of Christian doctrine offers precisely that opportunity.

Alister McGrath speaks of Christian doctrine as "the fabric that weaves Scripture together." He compares the task of biblical preaching with the craft of weaving: "A Scripture passage is a thread in the coat that doctrine weaves together."[15]

In 1994, the General Assembly of the Presbyterian Church (USA) declared, "Theology Matters." It remains to be seen how that body – and the council that is charged with implementing its will – understood the meaning of those words. But it is clear that among the congregations of this denomination there is a growing desire to study Christian doctrine, to discover what Christian brothers and sisters through the ages meant when they talked of such things as Incarnation, Trinity, and Communion. Excellent resources are being developed in order to meet this need, one of the finest recent examples being John H. Leith's *Basic Christian Doctrine*.[16] Leith's contribution interprets the history of Christian doctrine in language that is both contemporary and non-technical, thus providing a useful resource for the Christian laity, as well as for theological students and ministers.

This interest in Christian doctrine at the local church level is a significant sign of hope. In time, it will produce a laity that is better able to articulate the basics of Christian belief. In turn, the laity will expect greater theological competence from its ministers, and that expectation will alter theological curricula at the seminaries.

This chain of reforms will take time to bear fruit, but the good news is that it has already begun at the place where it matters most, in the congregations. Institutions and bureaucratic structures rarely lead reforms. But they must follow them. They must adapt to reforms arising out of local church communities – they must provide the services that are expected of them – or they will die as congregations turn elsewhere for resources that will meet their needs.

In Great Britain, reforms in theological education have forged ahead of their counterparts in the United States. Just as Britain preceded America's decline into secularism, so it appears to be leading in the long climb out. The doctrine of the Trinity has attracted some of the brightest minds in England and Scotland. Excellent studies are emerging from Ridley Hall in Cambridge, King's College in London, Wycliffe Hall at Oxford, and New College at Edinburgh. Handsel Press, located at Carberry Tower, a Christian retreat center near Edinburgh, is publishing first-rate pieces on Christian doctrine. The *Scottish Journal of Theology* has exposed its readers to outstanding evangelical scholarship. "Forward Together," a voluntary association of evangelical leaders in the Church of Scotland, is growing rapidly, providing encouragement and support for those who challenge heresy within the Christian community.

Graham Cray, Principal of Ridley Hall in Cambridge, says that the faculties in six of the twelve seminaries that train clergy for the Church of England are now solidly evangelical and that more than one half of all seminary students in Britain now identify themselves as evangelicals.[17] Citing statistics indicating that there are two million Christians now worshiping in Church of England sanctuaries each Sunday, Cray says attendance is on the rise. He reports that although many village churches, for practical reasons, have been closed, the Church of England is planting as many new churches as it is closing. The majority of senior clergy positions is still occupied by liberals, but these ministers are beginning to feel pressure as evangelical clergy serving smaller congregations nearby produce embarrassing comparative church attendance statistics. The Gospel is being preached in Great Britain, and the tide is beginning to turn.

SCIENCE AND FAITH: A RETURN TO STEREOSCOPIC VISION

Strange as it may seem, says Lesslie Newbigin, the physicists are ahead of the theologians.[18] The good news is that modern science has abandoned the mechanistic assumptions of Newtonian physics. Arguing that the Newtonian theory simply cannot account for molecular motion, James Clerk Maxwell demonstrated that one cannot explain the phenomenon of light by Newtonian physics. Additionally, and no less significantly, Albert Einstein showed us that Newton's strictures leave no room for theories of relativity.

Newbigin finds great promise in the work of Hungarian scientist Michael Polanyi, whose research on crystals in the 1930s led to important implications, not only for science, but for epistemology and theology. Polanyi insists on the falsity of the objective-subjective dualism that lies at the heart of Newtonian physics. His inquiries do for modern science what Nicaea did for theology. They bridge false dichotomies between spirit and matter, subject and object, knower and known.

As it has entered the nuclear age, modern science has found it necessary to cast aside the dualism implicit in Enlightenment philosophy. It finds the primary premise false. Thus, it is the contemporary scientist, not the theologian, who has called for a return to the Nicene world view. Meanwhile, establishment leaders of the mainline denominations continue to promote a threadbare theology that is based on discredited Enlightenment assumptions. The presuppositions that underlie their curriculum material and public pronouncements cling to the coattails of a world view that was popular when diseases were cured with leeches. Claiming to be contemporary, post-Enlightenment theologians who occupy tenured chairs in our seminaries are very much passé. While they were sleeping, the world turned. One of the Church's signs of hope – strange as it may seem to evangelicals who have often regarded science as a threat to faith – is emerging from the discoveries of modern science.

THE GROWTH OF EVANGELICALISM

In the United States, the explosive growth of nondenominational Christian churches has been truly remarkable. Although their styles of worship span the spectrum, one aspect of their message appears universal: The core of their Gospel is a personal relationship with Jesus Christ, Son of God, author of our salvation. On this point, they do not equivocate. That is the message that has built megachurches, both on the ground and in the airwaves, where evangelicals effectively utilize a powerful medium for proclaiming the Gospel to other people.

But there are also dangers in these developments that must not be overlooked. Megachurches, parachurches and other nondenominational communions often define themselves by their distance from tradition. They appeal to "baby boomers" and to "Generation X" by representing something new, vibrant, exciting, a place where "the Spirit" is alive, a place of emotional exhilaration. But, as we have seen, cutting oneself off from one's heritage means isolating oneself within a particular, and often private, emotional experience. At such moments, what happens to our accountability to that communion of the saints whose ties transcend our particular time and space? What happens to our knowledge of Christian doctrine, that conversation with the whole Church of Jesus Christ? Parachurch reluctance to take the history of Christian doctrine seriously can lead to gross excesses, cults, and rank commercialism, all in the name of Jesus.

Thus, while mainline Christians must recognize the growth of nondenominational evangelicalism – how can we ignore it? – we must also assess its impact with care. Clearly, the very existence of this movement points to a deficiency in the mainline's witness. Millions of people have left establishment denominations because they could detect no difference between these institutions and the culture that surrounded them. In lieu of a personal relationship with Jesus Christ, worshipers were offered politics and pop psychology, an ersatz gospel that left them hungry for spiritual food. Mainline church leaders must confess this sin, repent of it, connect once more with the faith of their forebears, and preach the Gospel with the power of revived conviction.

REFORMATION HAS BEGUN

Signs of hope abound among many congregations within America's mainline denominations. Members of these communions are rediscovering Scripture, conversing with their rich theological heritage, and developing societies of mutual support for the role they must play in their engagement with culture. That engagement is beginning, as they are now forcefully challenging their own denominational leaders to cease their assignations with an Arian Christ.

The reformation that has begun at the congregational level will ultimately wind its way to the top of the ecclesiastical pyramid. Resistance from national bureaucracies need not be a source of discouragement. Christians who know their history should expect and interpret opposition as did Athanasius on the eve of his fourth exile: " 'Tis but a little cloud, and soon it will pass." On the basis of what is already happening among congregations in America's mainline denominations, there is reason to hope for the emergence of denominational structures that will welcome the fervor of evangelical experience, tempered by a continuing accountability to the witness of the whole body of Christ.

LEARNING FROM NICAEA

Nicaea represented a defining moment in the history of the Christian Church. Bishops who gathered in that place – and those who continued the debate for the half-century that followed – were forced to choose between two saviors. The Emperor's conflict management schemes failed, for there could be no middle ground. Risking his ecclesiastical position, his reputation, and even his life, Athanasius stood firm against every scheme that would have compromised Jesus Christ, Son of God, of one essence with the Father.

But Nicaea is not only an event in the Christian past, for the question that ancient Council addressed is the Lord's question, and he directs it anew to each generation. Like Nicaea, we define ourselves and the institutions that we serve with our answer:

"Who do *you* say that I am?"

"You are the Christ, the Son of the Living God."

NOTES

1. We employ the term "mainline" in the traditional sense, as a designation for those Protestant ecclesiastical institutions that have for many years enjoyed an unofficial establishment status in American culture. These denominations, which include the Presbyterian Church (USA), the United Methodist Church, the Episcopal Church in America and the United Church of Christ, comprise the core of the politically active National Council of Churches.

   There are those who would question the adequacy of the term "mainline" for these groups today. Pointing to their plummeting memberships, internecine struggles, and eroding cash reserves, orthodox thinkers like Richard John Neuhaus prefer to speak of them as "old-line churches," a label that recognizes their claim to tradition but points to the fact that these institutions are being eclipsed by the vibrant growth of evangelical communions. For the same reason, others have adopted the term "side-line."

2. Moderator's Invitational Mission Forum, January 30, 1996, Louisville, Kentucky.

3. Augustine, *Confessions*, in *Basic Writings of Saint Augustine,* ed. Whitney J. Oates (New York: Random House, 1948), Vol. 1, p.3.

4. Judges 21:25.

5. To name an object is to define it, to circumscribe it with limits, to affirm dominion over it. That is precisely what those who insist on re-imagining God seek to accomplish. In naming God, they assume the role of God. They become God. The God who revealed himself to Moses would not be named. He identified himself as YHWH, the deity who transcends our definitions. He names us, and charges us, created in his image, to name the rest of creation.

6. Exodus 20:2-3.

7. I Peter 2:10 (Revised Standard Version).

8. John 1:14.

9. Matthew 16:16-18.

10. Hebrews 11:1 (King James Version), emphasis added.

11. Francis A. Schaeffer, *The God Who Is There* (Downers Grove: InterVarsity Press, 1968), p. 127.
12. Ibid.
13. The basis of apologetics is found in I Peter 3:15: "Always be ready to give a defense [*apologia*] to everyone who asks you for a reason for the hope that is in you."
14. Barely one-third of Presbyterian Church (USA) congregations purchase the denomination's official curriculum. In 1995, as had been the case in preceding years, curriculum production has resulted in huge deficits.
15. Interview at Wycliffe Hall, Oxford, October 7, 1994.
16. John H. Leith, *Basic Christian Doctrine* (Louisville: Westminster/John Knox Press, 1993).
17. Interview at Ridley Hall, Cambridge, October 4, 1994.
18. Interview in London, October 6, 1994.

SELECT BIBLIOGRAPHY

Allen, Diogenes. *Philosophy for Understanding Theology*. Atlanta: John Knox Press, 1985.

_____. *Three Outsiders: Pascal, Kierkegaard, Simone Weil*. Cambridge, Mass.: Cowley Publications, 1983.

Barnes, Timothy D. *Athanasius and Constantius: Theology and Politics in the Constantinian Empire*. Cambridge, Mass.: Harvard University Press, 1993.

Begbie, Jeremy. *Voicing Creation's Praise: Towards a Theology of the Arts*. Edinburgh: T&T Clark, 1991.

Bright, William, ed. *The Orations of St. Athanasius against the Arians according to the Benedictine Text*. Oxford: Clarendon Press, 1873.

Buckley, Michael. *At the Origins of Modern Atheism*. New Haven: Yale University Press, 1987.

Bultmann, Rudolf. *Jesus Christ and Mythology*. New York: Charles Scribner's Sons, 1958.

Coyne, Jr., John R. "Ultimate Reality in Chicago." The *Presbyterian Layman,* Nov/Dec. 1993.

Eastland, Terry, ed. *Religious Liberty In The Supreme Court: The Cases That Define the Debate Over Church and State*. Washington: Ethics and Public Policy Center, 1993.

Funk, Robert, et. al. *The Five Gospels: The Search for the Authentic Words of Jesus*. New York: Macmillan Publishing Co., 1993.

Gibbon, Edward. *The Decline and Fall of the Roman Empire*. New York: Random House, n.d.

Gregg, Robert C., and Groh, Dennis E. *Early Arianism: A View of Salvation*. Philadelphia: Fortress Press, 1981.

Gunton, Colin E. *Christ and Creation*. Grand Rapids: Wm. B. Eerdmans, 1992.

_____. *The Promise of Trinitarian Theology*. Edinburgh: T&T Clark, 1991.

Kelly, J.N.D. *Early Christian Creeds*, Third Edition. London: Longman Group, 1972.

_____. *Early Christian Doctrines*, Fifth Edition. London: A&C Black Ltd., 1977.

Johnson, Paul. *A History of Christianity.* New York: Simon & Schuster, 1976.

Jowett, B., trans. *The Dialogues of Plato, Vol. 1.* New York: Random House, 1920 (originally 1892).

Latourette, Kenneth Scott. *A History of Christianity.* New York: Harper and Row, 1953.

Leith, John H. *Basic Christian Doctrine.* Louisville: Westminster/John Knox Press, 1993.

Mays, James. "Comments on the Resurrection," *The Presbyterian Outlook,* April 22-29, 1996.

McGrath, Alister E. *Christian Theology: An Introduction.* Oxford: Blackwell Publishers, 1994.

McKeon, Richard, ed. *The Basic Works of Aristotle.* New York: Random House, 1941.

Newbigin, Lesslie. *A Faith For This One World?.* New York: Harper & Row, 1961.

_____. *Proper Confidence: Faith, Doubt, & Certainty in Christian Discipleship.* Grand Rapids: Eerdmans, 1995.

Oates, Whitney J. *Basic Writings of Saint Augustine.* New York: Random House, 1948.

Oden, Thomas. *Requiem.* Nashville: Abingdon Press, 1995.

Ottati, Douglas F. *Jesus Christ and Christian Vision.* Minneapolis: Fortress Press, 1989.

_____. "Meditation on Easter Sunday," *The Presbyterian Outlook,* April 1, 1996.

Patterson, Ben. "Heart and Soul." *Leadership Journal,* 16/2, Spring 1995.

Polkinghorne, John. *The Faith of a Physicist: Reflections of a Bottom-Up Thinker.* Princeton: Princeton University Press, 1994.

Ramm, Bernard L. *An Evangelical Christology.* Nashville: Thomas Nelson, 1985.

Schaeffer, Francis A. *The God Who Is There.* Downers Grove: InterVarsity Press, 1968.

_____. *Escape From Reason.* Downers Grove: InterVarsity Press, 1968.

Schaff, Phillip and Henry Wace, eds. *The Nicene and Post-Nicene Fathers.* Series I and II, 26 vols. New York: The Christian Literature Company, 1892.

Small, Joseph D., and John P. Burgess, "Re-Imagining: A Theological Appraisal," *The Presbyterian Outlook*, March 7, 1994.

Stevenson, J., ed. *A New Eusebius: Documents Illustrating the History of the Church To AD 337*. London: Cambridge University Press, rev. ed., 1987.

The Forgotten Trinity: 1 The Report of the BCC Study Commission on Trinitarian Doctrine Today. London: The British Council of Churches, 1989.

Torrance, Alan J. *Persons In Communion: An Essay on Trinitarian Description and Human Participation*. Edinburgh: T&T Clark, 1996.

Torrance, Thomas F. *The Trinitarian Faith*. Edinburgh: T&T Clark, 1993.

_____., ed. *The Incarnation: Ecumenical Studies in the Nicene-Constantinopolitan Creed*. Edinburgh: The Handsel Press, 1981.

Williams, Rowan. *Arius: Heresy and Tradition*. London: Darton, Longman and Todd Ltd., 1987.

Williamson, René de Visme. *Independence and Involvement: A Christian Reorientation to Politics*. Baton Rouge: Louisiana State University Press, 1964.